Bringing
Lucy
Home

Bringing
Lucy
Home

A Story of Hope,

Heartache,

and Happiness

Jennifer
Phillips

For Lucy, because you are worth it

and

For Dad, who was the first to say,
"You can do this."

Contents

Foreword

by Dr. Jere Phillips

Hope. All of us want it, but few people are willing to risk the heartache of hope delayed, hope rejected, hope denied. We like to play it safe. We accept normality without risk rather than reach for hope with the possibility of pain and failure.

God loves us enough to stretch our faith by calling us into ever-greater tests of trust. He sees beyond our imagination and invites us to follow His voice even though we cannot know where it leads. Such is the story of Jennifer and Lucy in *Bringing Lucy Home*.

Yonghui (Lucy) was born without hope. Her country forbade families from having more than one child. Second children, or first-born girl babies, were often aborted or abandoned. In His mercy, God led Yonghui's mother to place her at the door of a hospital where at least she would have a chance, if not a hope.

The orphanage where Yonghui spent the first fifteen months of her life had many children to help and few resources. The workers were challenged to help this special needs infant who weighed only four pounds. Unable to turn over, she lay flat on a board in a crib without mattress, sheet, blanket, or pillow. Even if she lived, she would grow up in an atheistic society with little opportunity to hear about Jesus, much less trust Him for salvation.

Where there is no hope, God intervenes with His providence in ways a little Chinese child could not imagine. Years before Yonghui's birth, God brought a young American college student to China. That student, Jennifer, witnessed firsthand the distress experienced by people like Yonghui's birth parents. Her heart broke at the drastic dilemma of these children and ultimately led her to consider giving one of those babies hope for the first time in her life.

This story, though, involves more than the hope of adoption. It is about the heartache Jennifer experienced as she found herself trapped in a bureaucratic quagmire that threatened Lucy's hope. Moreover, it is the narrative of how a young mother's faith was challenged and how she drew closer to her Heavenly Father through the process of pain.

You have to read the irony and humor in Jennifer's style to enjoy this story fully. People who know her can hear the smile in her voice as she tells some parts of the story. We can also hear the cry of pain as she confesses her struggles in other scenes.

As a father, I struggled alongside her. Her mother and I hurt to see her going through so much difficulty. We shared her fear when unreasonable governmental decisions threatened our new grandchild. At the same time, our faith was strengthened as we saw Jennifer work through the pain by the grace of God. In the end, we rejoiced to see God's presence, power, protection, and provision along each step of the way. Heartache finally yielded to happiness as Jennifer and Lucy ultimately were reunited with the rest of their family.

Her story could be your story. You may be struggling against hope. Your Heavenly Father may be calling you into deeper trust, stronger faith, higher hope.

Be prepared to laugh, cry, and come to the end of the story having worked past the temporary heartache to true happiness—the sum of our hope.

Introduction

I am not a bold person.

　　If someone were to read the story of my life, they might disagree. It appears on the surface as if I do bold things all the time. I always auditioned for church solos (and rarely got them, but that's beside the point). I was elected to leadership positions in school and spent one summer in China and another in Thailand. Following God's call to the mission field, I moved with my husband and children to Australia, literally as far away from family as one could possibly go.

　　There's a difference between *doing bold things* and *being bold,* as a character trait. I feel like my personality is a complex mix of wanting desperately to be a risk taker, yet being such a scaredy cat. I really want to be one of those people who are adventurous, competitive, and confident, not caring who's watching; but I'm just not. So, throughout my life, I've oscillated between avoiding situations that will put me in the limelight with the opportunity to fail, and purposefully putting myself in the spotlight (literally, if we're talking about karaoke). I make myself do frightening things, but inwardly tremble the whole time. Can anyone relate?

　　In college, when everyone was jumping off the sixty foot cliff into the lake, I made myself climb up, shaking the whole time, and jumped like the rest of them, but there was nothing at all about that experience that I found thrilling. I *hated it.* I totally played it cool, of course. Look at me! I'm such a risk taker! Oh, do I want to do it again? No, I'm good—my, uh, sciatica is acting up.

　　Another example: I've always loved to run, but I chickened out of running track in high school because the thought of people watching me run made me want to vomit. It's not like I would throw up and then blame it on how fast or far I just ran. I would probably actually vomit at the starting line.

Put me in a race of thousands, and I will be ultra-competitive because I blend in with the crowd. Random middle-aged woman running beside me who doesn't know my name, you are going down! Yet, if you ask me to race my husband with twenty people watching, because they want to see if I can beat him, my palms sweat at the mere thought of it. I refuse. For the record, I'm pretty confident I could beat him any distance past 200 meters, but we'll never know, now will we?

Don't get me started on that horrible "Steal the Bacon" schoolyard game I was subjected to as a child. You know the one. You stand in two lines on opposite ends of the field, eyeing a metal baton directly between the two lines. Each person has a number, and when your number is called, you and the kid in the other line with the same number race for the proverbial "bacon," as everyone else watches and plans to ridicule you for the rest of your life if you don't win. Let's not even consider the possibility of tripping. May as well change schools. You stand there in anxious agony, trying not to wet your pants while you pray that your number won't be called. Then you hear it: "17!" "NOOOOOOOOOO!!!!!" This is the point where my fear makes me run like crazy—like Phoebe from *Friends* crazy.

I apologize if I've dredged up traumatic childhood memories for you. I lead a support group on Thursday nights, if you're interested. Do not be ashamed, my friends.

The list goes on. I'd rather build on others' ideas than put my own thoughts forward. You'll never see me attempt to make any major fashion statements, at least not intentionally. I tend to choose paths I've seen others successfully walk instead of finding my own way. I love Girls' Nights Out, but wait on others to initiate the date instead of planning one myself. What if no one wants to go? It would be Girl (singular) Night Out, and that's not nearly as much fun, I don't care how introverted you are. I want to be bold, but it is not in my nature, however much I want it to be.

What about you? Maybe you are the type to go boldly into one adventure after another. You may engage uncertainty courageously with eager anticipation. Sorry, that's not me. I fight change with all my might, clinging to what's familiar until my hands ache, slip, and I'm hurled against my will towards the Big Black Hole of the Unknown.

How thankful I am that God pushes me off the Comfort Cliff, causing me to interact meaningfully with a world much bigger than the small circle I like to draw around myself. He leaves me with no choice but to trust Him as I free fall into depths of His character that I never would have known otherwise.

It was the free fall that led me to one of the greatest, most unexpected loves of my life. During a pivotal time of conviction in my life, God was saying, "Your dreams for your life and your family are too small. It's time to walk off the cliff." At that moment, a tiny four-pound baby was placed on the steps of a hospital in the still of the night, in a land far away. In a way, this baby and I were one in the same—fearful, left out in the great Unknown. Yet, we were different. She had been abandoned by the people who loved her most, but I was being pursued by the fierce love of my Heavenly Father who said, "Step out and trust me. Let's do this together, you and I."

So I took a step, rocks of familiarity crumbling beneath my feet, and I began to free fall towards this little one before I even knew her name. I had no idea that before landing on solid ground, I would face not only hardship and emotional turmoil, but unprecedented challenges played out on a national scale.

I had no idea that God would give me such a story to tell. At times, I begged Him for another story. Now that I know the ending, I'm so thankful He did not. It's a story that has been a privilege to live out, and is now a privilege to share, as I marvel at the precious life God redeemed and restored.

This, my friends, is the story of Bringing Lucy Home.

Chapter 1

The Road to Hope

The road to hope often has strange beginnings. A tiny Chinese girl, abandoned shortly after birth, found her way to a loving home by way of winding trail that started with an American college sophomore's struggle to prove herself. I'm tempted to lie and say that my story has a noble beginning, something like, "From the time I could talk, I've been broken for the plight of orphans, and I knew that one day, *one day*, I would adopt."

Actually, my story begins with a decision made out of spite. The year was 1998. *Wasn't that like yesterday?* I was dating my future husband, Brian. We both were involved with a Christian college organization and were part of its core leadership team. Each year, a handful of students were asked to participate in a summer-long cross-cultural project, and I felt like this was my year. The trip was to Japan, and I thought that would be just awesome. The time came for the students to be chosen. My two best friends were picked. Brian was picked. I was not.

Um, I'm sorry, but somehow it must have been overlooked that I am a pastor's daughter, and I've been a Christian since I was six years old. I've led many Bible studies, and I am more than qualified for this trip. I was *fired up.*

My first reaction was anger and jealousy because Brian was chosen but I wasn't. He had never even participated in Bible Drill, for Heaven's sake! Anger turned to bitterness, which led to "I'll show them." My university was offering a trip to Xi'an, China, to teach English and basketball to inner city junior high kids, and I thought that was my chance.

I was so desperate to show that "I can go overseas, too" that I actually signed up to teach basketball. You're talking about someone who played church league basketball for eight years and still couldn't dribble correctly. My friends called me Yoshi because I stuck my neck out so far when I ran down the court. My career high was five points in one game, and I celebrated like I'd just clinched the NBA Finals. Basketball coach material, for sure.

I love how God accomplishes His purposes despite our wrong motivations. In Philippians, Paul basically says, "What does it matter that some people share the gospel out of wrong motivations? At least Christ is preached!" (Philippians 1:15-18). I can relate, Paul. My motivations for wanting to go to China may have begun selfishly, but God actually used my stubborn pride to get me on a trip I was meant to go on all along. I would not understand His reasons until fifteen years later.

As often is the case, God gently convicted me of my pride, softened my heart, and I was able to rejoice in Brian's opportunity to go to Japan. I also got excited about the possibility of loving under-privileged Chinese children, and teaching them the art of a really bad lay-up. Right now in China, there are about a hundred people in their late twenties who think you actually shoot a free-throw granny-style. I'm guilt-stricken.

My month in China was beautifully life changing. I had never been out of the United States before, so I was enamored with everything. The sights, the sounds, the smells—oh, the smells. July in Xi'an was sweltering, and I can't say the city's sanitation methods (aka, leaving trash on the curbside to rot in the humidity) were the most efficient or pleasant. Nor was the chicken head that stared up at me from my plate during my birthday dinner, daring me to be so cruel as to eat him while he was still looking at me. I declined.

Our mornings were spent teaching English as a Second Language—and basketball—at an impoverished school. Afternoons often involved meeting our students' families. It was such a humbling experience to be invited into a home consisting of four cinder block walls, especially since we walked there from our five-star hotel. Our hosts insisted we sit on the bed, which was the only piece of furniture in the room, while they sat on the floor. They served us simple meals that probably cost them a day's wages, and were happy to do it.

When I looked into the eyes of my new Xi'an friends, I saw hardship, yet wisdom; a love of family and community, yet deep sorrow for what they and their countrymen endured.

During this trip I was introduced to the One Child Policy. Family and ancestry are sacred to the Chinese culture, yet most of my students had no brothers or sisters. I probably had heard of China's form of population control, but now I was confronted with its reality face-to-face. As a young twenty-one-year-old, still very much self-absorbed, I did not explore the harsh consequences this policy created. I don't think I dwelled much on the possibility of babies abandoned by the thousands, or many more children lost to voluntary and forced abortions. I didn't think about the preference of sons over daughters, or healthy children versus the handicapped or frail. I didn't ponder how lessening the value of life can devastate a culture.

Here were the seeds I took away from that trip—seeds that germinated over the next decade and a half of my life: The Chinese are a gracious, generous people. Through others' decisions, these truly lovely people are forced to abandon their own flesh and blood, or worse. This reality is crushing for them.

I wanted to help, but what could I do at twenty-one and still in school? Nothing at the time. Yet through English lessons and dribbling drills and shared cups of hot tea in even hotter crowded street shops, through listening, smiling, and gazing into wise, ancient eyes, a love and compassion for the Chinese settled into my heart, creating space and desire for a fragile Lianjiang treasure that would enter my life many years later.

First, I had to decide what to do with my life.

Did you know that procrastination is an art form? It takes mad skills to put off extremely important decisions, and then actually pull through at the last second.

Putting things off is the story of my life, and the pattern usually goes something like this: Procrastinate any decision either until someone makes the decision for you, or you've procrastinated so long that you're only left with one option, so that's the one you choose! Brilliant, if you ask me, although I don't recommend this strategy to my own children, because the system eventually breaks down.

As college graduation approached with the subtlety of a freight train, my casual uncertainty about what I would do with my life quickly turned to panic. I had declared psychology as a major at the last minute. I had no idea what I'd do with it, but just wanted to help people. So young, so naïve, so didn't choose a major that is especially marketable long-term without a higher degree. At least I could help people, right? Um, it's more like I could help them through the door of the unemployment office as I followed behind. Darn it, Younger Self! Why didn't you choose Pharmacy??

After turning down an opportunity to go to grad school (you're killing me, Younger Self), I found myself with a college degree, an apartment, roommates, a soon-to-be fiancé, and no job. I literally started flipping through the Yellow Pages, which isn't the most strategic way to find employment, but you have to start somewhere. My recently graduated and jobless best friend and I referred to this period of our lives as "Reality Bites."

When the Yellow Pages turned out to be a dead end (shocking!), my sister suggested I look into her line of work. She was a social worker at an adoption agency, loved it, and thought I would too. I would be helping people! "I've heard good things about a place called

Sav-A-Life," she said, referring to a Christian crisis pregnancy center close to where I lived. I flipped through the still-open Yellow Pages, found the number, and cold-called them.

As Providence would have it, who answered the phone but a friend of mine whom I hadn't been in contact with for several years. We reconnected immediately. When I revealed I was a recent grad looking for a job, she lit up. "Our board just approved a full-time receptionist position! Do you want to apply?"

Ahem.

What I wanted to say was, "I'm sorry, but I just worked my tail off for the last four years, at great cost to my parents, to graduate summa cum laude from a distinguished private university. I've got higher learning skills. I don't *do* phones." What I said instead was, "Great! I'll think about it." In other words, "Don't call me, I'll call you."

Once again my pride was wounded, and I dismissed the offer. Thankfully, God would not allow me to let it go. The job was on my mind constantly, and every other opportunity I pursued ended with a closed door. It was the strongest I've ever felt God say, "If you don't do this, you're being disobedient." Righty-o. I guess I'm in. I called and arranged an interview.

Armed with my resumé hot off the press, and attempting to look as professional as I'd seen people in the movies appear when interviewing for a job, I walked into the brick building hopeful, yet still disappointed about the whole receptionist thing. As the Executive Director laid out the vision of the ministry and the statistics of women and children whose lives had been saved through the years, I was won over. I thought, "My role may be small, but this is a cause I can throw my heart into: caring for the defenseless, loving women, sharing Christ. Let's do this."

I was not a fantastic receptionist because I kept leaving my post to talk to the people in the waiting room. I couldn't help myself. We offered free pregnancy testing, so each person who walked through our doors had one thing in common: they either thought they were pregnant, or they were with someone who did. Each girl's story was unique. Some women were brimming with excitement over the possibility of having a baby. Others were terrified, mortified, or in shock. I wanted to hear their stories.

I offered cups of water to the shaky sixteen-year-old girl, and then talked to her even shakier boyfriend after she went back for her test and counseling. I comforted the devastated mom of a pregnant teen. I had the privilege of sharing the hope of Jesus with countless people from all walks of life. This experience was wonderful for my desire to help people, but terrible for my actual job description. The phones rolled over to voicemail way more times than they should during business hours.

After only working a few months, the position of Volunteer Coordinator opened up. My boss gladly took me off the neglected front desk, and placed me in a role that I loved—training, organizing, and encouraging volunteers, and counseling clients who felt as if they were out of options. My greatest joys during this time period included leading women into a personal relationship with Jesus and seeing lives saved.

My first personal exposure to adoption came from the perspective of the birth mother. I talked to countless girls about adoption during my years at Sav-A-Life, where I eventually served as Executive Director. I championed adoption as a selfless alternative to pregnancy termination, and truly, it is. I witnessed success stories of young women who courageously chose to place their children with loving families. I knew it was hard on the birth mother, but because I knew that it was sometimes the right thing for both mother and baby, I could promote adoption as a wonderful option.

I thought I had an understanding of a birth mother's pain, but it was not until I had my first child that it hit me full force. I will never forget that miraculous moment when the doctor laid Joshua on my chest. He and I were one, and I loved him with a ferocity that I had never experienced. From that first second, I would have laid down my life for him.

It wasn't until the enormity of that moment that I understood how excruciating it would be to hand over your own child for someone else to mother. *I cannot imagine the pain.* I cannot conceive looking into those beautiful, trusting eyes, stroking that soft cheek, and saying good-bye. Holding my son, I realized the heartache a mother might experience who would never witness the "firsts" with her child, who would visualize someone else comforting him in the middle of the night, who would know that he would call someone else "Mama." It was just too much to grasp.

These women are heroes in my book, placing the needs of their children above their own and making the ultimate sacrifice. Adoption is heartbreakingly beautiful. I wish I could go back to each of those women whom I, barely out of school, counseled towards the choice of adoption. I would like to say, "I thought I understood what you were going through, but I really had no idea. Please forgive me if I somehow did not love you well enough during that time." I would love to say thank you, and tell them again how proud I am of them for doing something I don't know that I would have the courage to do if I found myself in the same situation.

I wish I could tell them I didn't know it at the time, but their stories would one day weave into my own story. Witnessing their heartache would fuel my compassion for a faceless, nameless woman in a poor Chinese city who was brave enough to give her baby a chance at life the best way she knew. I would love for them to know that seeing the raw pain in their eyes opened my own eyes to the hope that this baby was not merely a crowded country's castaway, but the daughter of someone who paid the greatest cost so her child might possibly be saved.

Chapter 2

Down Under

So, what does China have to do with Australia, where we live now? Brian and I married in the spring of 2000, and, boy, did we have big plans. He was working for the same ministry in which we were both heavily involved during college. We had dreams of living overseas one day, but later discovered it was easy to fantasize about living in a third world country, laying our lives down for the sake of the gospel, when it was just the two of us. What an adventure! The more difficult the living conditions, the better!

Two-and-a-half years into marriage, we found out we were having a son. Game changer. At least for me. Brian was still all, "Let's move to Africa and live in a hut!" and I was backpedaling as fast as my pregnant self could go. "I don't know, B—I mean, I'm pretty sure God's calling us to stay in Birmingham for the rest of our lives." While he was investigating seminaries in the Philippines and writing papers on why India would be the most strategic place to live, I was looking into extending our mortgage.

Funny story about India:

One day, Brian enthusiastically presented me with a DVD featuring India and its need for the gospel. He asked me to watch it and tell him what I thought. I begged off that night with a headache, but promised to watch it soon. Each day, he would come home and ask if I watched the video. My answers ranged from "The baby cried all day," to "I think I'm suffering from post-partum, and it would make me too sad," to "I think the baby ate the DVD," to "Yeah, I didn't want to." I refused to watch the video.

Who does that? Who refuses to watch a video about the plight of a country because she is afraid if she watches it, her husband might think she actually wants to live there? This. Girl. I also declared that I would never move to a country that ended in "stan," as in Paki*stan*, Kazakh*stan*, Tajiki*stan*. If you end in "stan," you are a dangerous country and therefore no place for my newborn child and me. The end. (*Disclaimer: I am so thankful for missionaries who move to places like India and the "stan" countries. I'm sure they are beautiful countries with needy people. Those missionaries are so much braver than I. I'm gutless, what can I say?*)

This issue of moving overseas continued to be a major source of contention in our marriage over the next five years. With each child—first Joshua, then Andrew, then Sarah Kate—I dug in my heels and sank my roots deeper in the friendly South. I loved being close to family, dear friends, and my best friend living two doors down from me. Life was good; why go and mess it up? My vehement resistance shot down every option Brian pursued. I did not want to move overseas, and I could not see how we would ever be on the same page about it. Lots of tears and harsh words were exchanged over this topic. It was hard.

In the spring of 2007, Brian was invited to accompany his boss on a vision trip to Australia. Brian had never considered Australia because it seemed too "soft." I mean, how can you suffer for Jesus on the Sunshine Coast? Let's be honest. You can't, really. Still, not one to turn down a free trip to Australia, he said "yes" to a visit he didn't consider to be much more than a vacation.

God did something pretty amazing in Brian's heart during his week in Brisbane. He pulled back the veneer of the staggering physical beauty of a country on everyone's bucket list, and showed him the thirst of a nation on the verge of utter spiritual deadness. He discovered a people with great need they did not realize they had. God also convicted him of his pride for thinking the harder a place is to live, the more spiritual and strategic it is. Just because Australia has some killer beaches doesn't mean God cannot call you and use you there.

Brian fell in love with the people and the culture, and his heart broke over their need for Christ. A running joke in our family is that Brian wanted to go to Australia all along, but he used threatening words like India to trick me into agreeing to move Down Under.

Brian: "Jennifer, I think God's calling us to India."
Me: "Over my dead body."
Brian: "How about Australia then?"
Me: "Sounds good!"

It didn't really go like that, but one way God confirmed we were supposed to move to Australia was that for the first time in five years of conversation and conflict, we were on the same page. I still was not happy about living literally as far as you could possibly go from family and friends, but I knew it was right.

The theme of the months leading up to our big move was Sad with a capital S. I grieved for a year and a half, and the grief got more intense the closer we came to our departure date. I just could not imagine being so far away from our parents—the kids' grandparents. There wouldn't be sleepovers at Nana and PaPaw's, and we would miss out on Uncle Eddie's smoked ribs at Christmas, for Pete's sake! No more little cousins giggling together at family gatherings; no more road trips with my sister. I felt like we were heading into the Black Hole, and Life as I Knew It was dying a slow, painful death.

The Day arrived far too quickly. We sobbed our way through an airport scene I never want to repeat, and stepped onto a four hundred and fifty-six hour plane ride that would take us to our new home. Okay, maybe it was just twenty-six, but when you're traveling across the world with a seven year old, a five year old, and a three year old, you have permission to exaggerate because perception is, in fact, reality.

We adored Brisbane from the start. It is a stunning city, with huge parks, even larger tropical birds, and a winding river you can travel via water taxi. How cool is that? How many kids from Alabama get to hop on a boat and ride to the man-made beach on the other side of the river for a day of fun and sun, while multicolored birds the size of their heads flock above in the cornflower blue sky? The weather is gorgeous ninety percent of the time, and you are an hour away from the coast, mountains, and water parks—my personal favorite. There is a reason why Australia is on everyone's bucket list.

However, I had some trouble adjusting. I was sadder than sad, missing people I loved back home. Too, we ran into some cultural differences that I had a tough time getting used to, such as spiders the size of your face that for some reason saw a green light to roam freely throughout people's homes.

One night was particularly traumatic. Brian was out of town, and I was all snuggled in bed, exhausted from a long day with the kids sans Dad, when the thought crossed my mind, "Did I lock the back door?" Groan. I guess I'll go look. Checked the door, and of course it was locked because I'm OCD about that kind of stuff. As I sleepily walked toward my bedroom, something dark caught my eye. The biggest, ugliest spider I have ever seen in my life was on the wall over the entrance to my bedroom. I'm talking, bigger than my hand big, and unlike any spider I had seen to date. I would post a picture, but I know my Mom will never come visit me again. You'll just have to use your imagination.

"Brian!!! Come kill this—" Oh wait. You're not here. "Joshua!!" No, you're eight, and you're asleep. So, that leaves me as the only one who can do something about this situation. I pondered my options. I didn't want to smash it, because it was so big and fat. I just could not bring myself to do it. The only other option was to spray it with insect killer and hope it would crumple and die.

After I took a picture to document my assassin, I climbed on a chair, spray in hand, aimed, and missed. He fell to the ground and RAN INTO MY BEDROOM. Enter hysterics. I started yelling, "Oh, Lord Jesus! Oh, Lord Jesus! Help!" I watched as Ugly ran behind a filing cabinet. Aha! I'll use my brute strength and smash him with the filing cabinet! Nope, he's too fast and RUNS UNDERNEATH THE BED!!! Noooooo!!! We had about ten suitcases under our bed—a spider's hide and seek dream come true. I was doomed.

Okay, first things first. As an initial line of defense, I ran to my closet and, despite the fact that it was ninety degrees outside and our house was not air-conditioned, I put my snow boots on. I'm sure I had a perfectly good reason for bringing snow boots to Australia; I just can't remember it right now. So, snow boots: check. Next step, call someone. It's 11:30 p.m. Who can I call, who can I call? Aha! 7:30 a.m. in America, baby. My sister is up getting kids ready for school! I call her in a panic. I think she heard something like, "Ahhhhhhhh!!!! Spider—bed— ugly—is going to kill me— ahhhhh!!!!!!"

After she had a freak out session of her own, she started to give me advice. Um, what advice is there to give other than put your snow boots on? Well, she had some, the first suggestion being that I should kick the suitcases and try to get him to run out, because how am I ever going to sleep again if I don't find him? So, snow boots secure, I kicked the fire out of those suitcases, and it worked, too, because he eventually came out.

I spotted him on the wall behind my nightstand. I didn't have much room to work with, but thought maybe I could get a book back there and smush him. Ew!! (Spoken as Jimmy Fallon's character Sara, with no "h.") I told Julianne I was putting the phone down, and to call the Australian police if I didn't come back. I got my book, took aim. Yet again, the beast was too fast. He ran down the wall and under the bed again. Blast!!!!

At this point, my sister took her advice to the next level, and I lost all sense of sanity. She said, "You need to tell that spider who's boss! Let him know who he's up against!" Now, I can't explain why this was the first thing that came into my mind, but I just started yelling, "I'm kind, I'm smart, and I'm important! Take that, Fur Legs!" My spider remained an unimpressed no-show.

Two hours later, after pulling everything out from under the bed, pacing around the room, and keeping vigil, I spotted movement. Ol' Eight Legs came crawling out from behind the bedpost and made himself comfy by the post under the bed. It was the least accessible place possible. He may have been a genius but it was one a.m. and I was desperate. Determined not to be defeated again, I chose my weapon carefully: a golf club. Pretty sure it was a driver—maybe a wedge—actually, I have no clue. I lay on my stomach under the bed, aimed, and with a guttural yell comparable to Mel Gibson's *Braveheart* battlecry, I obliterated that son of a gun.

Victory!!! After two hours of my screaming and stalking, the beast was dead. My adrenaline kept me awake for most of the night after that, but at least I wasn't worried about being poisoned in my sleep.

What were the life takeaways from this traumatic event?

1. Always smash the spider when you have the chance, no matter how fat he is. He thinks insect spray is a joke.
2. Don't ever let Brian leave town again.
3. Never rent a house across the street from the bush (that's "forest" in Australian). The lovely view is a façade for death and destruction.
4. Always pack your snow boots, even if you live in a semi-tropical climate. You never know when they just might save your life.

In addition to fearing the treacherous wildlife, we made a few sacrifices by moving Down Under. Some might seem trivial, like sweet tea and Chick-fil-A (okay, let's be honest—those examples are anything but trivial), but others were really tough, like leaving family, traditions, and the wonderful school our children attended.

One major desire that we thought we were laying down was the longing to adopt. We had talked adoption throughout our marriage, thinking how wonderful it would be to offer a child a forever family one day. However, one baby was born, then another, then another, and then we decided to not only move across the world from a strong support system, but we chose to move to a country with one of the lowest adoption rates in the world.

To say that adoption in Australia is rare is an understatement. In 2012, Australia granted only 339 adoptions nationwide, including international and domestic adoptions.[1] In that same year, the United States documented 8,668 international adoptions alone.[2] A massive difference.

Adoption is a sore subject for Australians. Why? The main reason is the Stolen Generation. In the early 1900's, in an act of what could be described as ethnic cleansing, the Australian government ordered the removal of thousands of aboriginal and Torres-Strait Islander children from their parents. Some of these little ones were adopted into white families, but most were raised in institutions, their identities lost forever.[3] These inhumane abductions occurred for the next *sixty years*.

During this same time period, single motherhood was so taboo that many women were coerced or tricked into placing their babies for adoption. Nurses would often give women adoption papers to sign while they were still under heavy sedation. The new mothers would wake up childless, their babies swept away to two-parent, "deserving" families.[4]

Can you even imagine the horror?

This was a dark, dark time in Australian history, and the repercussions still resonate throughout the culture. The Australian government has made formal apologies, but words cannot undo the decades of wrongdoing and loss. You can understand why the word "adoption" isn't the warm and fuzzy buzz word it is in the States. It is polarizing, to say the least.

In reaction to these atrocities, the Australian government swung to the opposite end of the spectrum by taking the position that it is almost always best for a child to stay with its mother, or at least in its own culture. State-by-state quotas were also placed on the number of international adoptions allowed each year.[5] Australians now wait six, eight, or sometimes ten years to adopt a child. Sometimes, after waiting as long as a decade, they are then told "no."

As I said, adoption is a sore subject for Australians.

So, when we knew we were moving to Brisbane, we thought we were saying good-bye to any dreams we ever had of adopting. I remember just a few days before we moved; I couldn't help myself from scrolling through photos of waiting orphans in China, desperately needing a family. I just did not want to let the dream go.

After we moved, every so often, I would Google "Can-Americans-living-in-Australia-adopt," because Google knows all, right? I usually didn't get very far, but one night, I followed a link to an agency whose sole purpose is to facilitate adoptions for Americans living overseas. I sent them a message explaining our situation and asked if they could help. They replied within a few days: "Yes." We were still permanent residents of the USA and could adopt through an American agency. I will never forget reading those words. Shivers ran down my spine.

I called my sister in a panic. "This guy is saying we can do this, but we have to do it *now*. Like, NOW." If you recall, I'm the girl who isn't bold, who is slow to change, who likes to consider an idea for a good long while, and takes eons to make a decision. We basically had a few weeks to decide whether or not we would pursue a child, instead of fantasizing about the possibilities. Our dream was being revived, and even though I was beside myself with excited disbelief, I also wanted to throw up from anxiety.

As I searched my heart before the Lord to see if this was what He wanted us to do, I found my old friend Fear. Fear of how such a decision would change our family. Fear of how adoption would affect our children. Fear of the emotional, physical, and financial sacrifices. Fear of the unknowns, of "doing hard."

When I thought back to sixteen months prior when we left all that we loved and moved to a foreign land, when I thought of the grief and stress we walked through, the depth of the pain I felt in letting go, I thought, "Oh Lord, we just 'did hard.' We did hard, and there were times I thought I wouldn't survive the grief. And You want us to shake things up again? Turn our family upside down again? We've just gotten to a good, solid place. We would be fools to take such a risk, wouldn't we?"

I worried about not having enough of me to offer Joshua as he headed into the tween years. I worried about the child not bonding to us. I worried about the trauma we could possibly cause our new child by making her an American, who's Chinese, who speaks with an Aussie accent! Talk about confused! I worried that Sarah Kate would despise her because she would have straight hair, the one thing SK has always wanted!!

Countless times my fears got the best of me and I wanted to walk away, to leave it to someone else, another mom who's braver, more patient than me. Yet each time, God would bring something or someone to confirm yet again what He was calling us to. I asked Sarah Kate, "If you had a sister, what would you want her name to be?" She said the exact name Brian and I had talked about only a few days before. In another instance, I received this verse in an email from a friend who had no idea what we were considering: "… *we pray always for you, that our God would count you worthy of this calling, and fulfill all the good pleasure of His goodness, and the work of faith with power: That the name of our Lord Jesus Christ may be glorified in you, and you in Him, according to the grace of our God and the Lord Jesus Christ*" (2 *Thessalonians 1:11*).

Brian, the calm, levelheaded member of our marriage, led me through a process of weighing pros and cons and praying through our options. I was so relieved to hear him say, "We make this decision together. This isn't your dream; it's our dream. If this ends up being extremely hard, this is a decision we made together. I'm on board 100%." After wrestling for days, I made this list:

Why do I want to adopt from China?

- *I've never felt like our family was complete, but have always felt like another little girl was missing.*
- *All orphans in China are abandoned. Placing your child for adoption is illegal, so babies are abandoned in hope that someone will find them and take them to an orphanage. Why NOT give one of them a home?*
- *God calls us to care for the orphans and the widows.*
- *A direct application of mercy ministry. I can only imagine the invaluable lessons the kids will learn about God's love for us and caring for others, especially those who can't care for themselves.*
- *As challenging as I know it will be, and as weak as I know I am as a mom, a life with us will be a million times better for this child than a lifetime in an orphanage, and then on to who knows what.*
- *Because I believe that God is a big God! If He is in this, He can overcome any legal or financial obstacle! The huge cost for the process is NOTHING to Him! We have been teaching the kids about God's promises to Abraham, and how He chooses the weak to do great things so that He will get the glory. In that same way, I feel like God could receive so much glory in how He carries this story out—how He made it possible for a not rich family living in Australia to adopt a little girl from China!*
- ***Because there is a little girl in an orphanage in China who needs us to be her forever family.***

So, on a late April morning, sitting on a park bench and considering this list, Brian and I said, "Let's go for it." With that decision, the process of bringing Lucy home officially began.

Chapter 3

The Curse of Detail Deficiency Disorder

I am pretty sure we annihilated an entire forest of trees with the paperwork required for our adoption. I had heard about document overload, but had no idea! For a person who is not, shall we say, detail oriented (more on that later), it was a major chore. In addition to the paperwork were the required millions of hours of adoption education, medical checks, blood work, and the biggie, The Home Study. The Home Study is the part where a family is picked apart brick-by-brick to see if there is any evidence of instability.

Uh-oh.

I knew I should have prepped Brian before our first home study visit by the local social worker. Brian loves to joke around, usually sarcastically, and doesn't always have a clear pulse on what's appropriate. I thought, surely, *surely* he knows this is a major deal so he'll be on his best behavior. (I think we all know where this is going. Think of the movie *What to Expect When You're Expecting*, and we'll be on the same page.)

All was going well. I was waxing poetic about the greatness of parental bliss, and Brian piped in with, "Well, let's be honest; kids are great, MOST of the time." At this point I silently mouthed, "Shut up!" Did he stop? Oh no. Brian: "Yeah, we don't really know what we fought about before we had kids! Heh Heh!!" Sharp kick to Brian's shin. Social worker remains stone faced. I expect her to start scribbling furiously while asking, "Yes, tell me more about the arguing." Enter me with over-compensating, cheesy gushing over the fact that *Children. Are. A. Blessing*!!! We love them! All the time! And they never fight! And we never fight! No, ma'am we do not.

Somehow, our marriage survived, and we got the green light as acceptable adoptive parents. It was on to the next hurdle: biometric fingerprints, which brings me back to that issue of details.

"Details, Jennifer, Details."

I cannot tell you how many times my Dad said this to me growing up, and with good reason. Details have never been my thing. Well, let me clarify. SOME details are my thing. I could memorize entire chapters of my AP Biology book, including captions under photos (got the top score on my AP Biology exam—holla!), I've been Executive Director of a non-profit organization, and I've been employed as a church administrator.

Academic details? Got it. Common sense details? Not so much. If you think about it, common sense would be a lot more useful to me than, to this day, knowing the function of the golgi apparatus. Lack of common sense details have led to the following scenarios throughout my life (and this is not even close to an exhaustive list, trust me):

- I drove through a car wash with my window down. The really bad thing was that it took me a few seconds to realize where the water was coming from. My windshield must be cracked! Is there a hole in the roof? Who opened my window?? I believe the correct description for my appearance was drowned rat. This happy event happened on my way back to college, and, unfortunately, I was minutes away from seeing Brian for the first time in six weeks. Thankfully, he's a fan of the "natural" look.

- I tried to pump gas one time, got really frustrated that it wasn't working, and tried to go inside to complain. At that point, I realized the gas station was under construction—as in it was *still being built*. No wonder there was no line, and no parking places, and no people.
- I once accidentally drove into the "correct change only" toll lane in Atlanta, during rush hour, and had to get out of my car and ask the guy behind me if I could borrow five cents, as if I could really repay him. He was soooo happy about that.
- Confident in my newfound knowledge of the metric system after living in Australia for only a few months, I decided to try my hand at ordering my deli meat in grams. Glancing side to side to make sure the Aussies standing beside me could hear how culturally aware my American self was, I loudly asked for "five hundred kilos of turkey, please" (wink to the lady next to me). For all of you who are metrically impaired, 500 kilos equals more than 1,000 pounds. The deli worker gave me an "Americans are morons" stare and asked, "What, did you win the lottery or something?" Realizing my mistake I replied, "Yes, and I really like turkey."

My next example is prize worthy if you ask me:

On an ordinary trip to my usual choice of grocery store, I retrieved a cart, started putting my items in, and noticed a crunching feeling under my feet. Immediately I thought, "This place is disgusting. How dirty!" I continued to crunch through the store, thinking the whole time that someone should really clean up this filthy establishment. After strolling down every single aisle, I pulled into the checkout line and heard the loud *whiirrrrrrr* of a vacuum cleaner. Well, it's about time. Then, I noticed the worker was driving the industrial-sized cleaning machine straight towards me, and right into my checkout lane. What in the world?

It was at this moment that I looked down and eyeballed the *empty five-pound bag of sugar in the front of my cart.* Oops. Sugar was one of the first items I grabbed, and apparently the bag was punctured. Like a faulty hourglass, I had been leaking sugar throughout the whole store, and walking right through it. *Crunch, crunch, crunch.*

I sheepishly picked up the empty bag, looked at the worker, and in the most charming voice I could muster said, "Uh, I just saw this." (*Insert nervous laughter.*) No smiles. Only firey "You're-an-idiot-and-made-my-day-so-much-harder" darts coming from her eyes. So, I take it you are *not* going to get me another bag of sugar? Right. I didn't need it anyway. I'll be leaving now.

The list could go on and on. It's demoralizing. I haven't even mentioned the 436 scrapes and scratches I've put on our cars because of my lack of depth perception. I have actually been stripped of my keys to our larger, newer car because I cannot cope. I'm only allowed to drive the beat-up Camry. Brian is trying to save me—and our budget—from myself.

Details, details. They are highly overrated. EXCEPT when your Detail Deficiency Disorder strikes a matter that's a really big deal, and the consequences are costly to yourself and others.

Can anyone say Lost Fingerprints?

One of the adoption requirements unique to us since we live in Australia was that our biometric fingerprinting had to happen at the U.S. Consulate in Sydney, which is ten hours away from where we live. Now, there are worse things than being required to travel to Sydney. I mean, I basically pretended I was a part of "Oprah Goes Down Under" as I gawked at the iconic Opera House, rode a ferry under the Harbor Bridge, and strolled through Hyde Park like a Boss. Brian and I might as well have been Keith and Nicole.

In addition to the fun, there was also a lot of cost involved in getting these fingerprints: the cost of plane tickets, hotel room, meals, and the cost of time invested by our kind friends who cared for our children while we were away. Oh, yes, let's not forget the actual cost of the fingerprints. We were happy to cover these costs, as it would push us one step closer to bringing our little girl home.

Our trip to Sydney was a success, and we were given the fingerprints in a sealed envelope to mail back to our adoption agency in the States. I posted the prints, task completed. Or so I thought. Several weeks later, the fingerprints had not arrived in the States. Our social worker asked for the tracking number so she could check on them. Uh oh. I suddenly realized I had made a huge mistake. In an effort to complete the task as quickly as possible, I never thought to send the prints by registered mail. Nor did I send them courier express. Nor did I put a return address on them, as the return address on the envelope given to us simply said, "U.S. Government," and everyone knows who they are, right?

If the prints were lost, there would be no way to recover them, and we would have to go back to Sydney and repeat the process, and pay the costs, all over again. We began to pray, and asked others to pray. Each morning I woke up and checked my email, hoping to receive confirmation of the prints' arrival. Each morning, I was disappointed.

I felt as if I had let everyone down. I let my husband and my family down, as lost prints would mean a great deal of money just thrown away. I let myself down—how could I have been so careless with something so dear? Most of all, I felt like I had let our little girl down. Lost prints meant further delay, and more of her days spent in an orphanage without a family.

Then I got a taste of grace. Grace from my husband, who didn't hold this over my head but told me it was okay. Grace from family and friends who offered to help logistically and financially should we need to visit Sydney again. Grace from the Lord, who reminded me that He is sovereign, even over my careless mistakes.

Grace was then applied in the most unexpected way. After four weeks of praying, we were resigned to buying plane tickets and returning to Sydney. But then we received the message we had been anticipating. Our fingerprints had arrived! Praise God! We were so relieved. I didn't deserve for God to intervene and grant me the desires of my heart, but He did it anyway. Grace applied.

Ah, Detail Deficiency Disorder, or as they call it in academic circles, Triple D. It attacks the best of us when we least expect it, because let's face it; we're not really paying attention anyway. I am thankful for friends and family who shake their heads and love me despite my unfortunate condition, and I'm grateful that God graciously fills in the gaps that my absent-mindedness inevitably creates.

Thank goodness, He *is* paying attention.

Chapter 4

The Costly Thing

Months of preparation came to an end as the most labor-intensive part of the adoption process for us was finally completed. All the paperwork was done, submitted to China, and then the real wait began—the wait to be matched with a child.

We knew it would take time to get The Phone Call. We were comfortable with waiting. We focused on investing in our other three kids, knowing their boats would be rocked soon enough. While thoughts of our daughter-to-be were never far from our minds, life was consumed with soccer practices and piano, school and church, and the millions of things in between. I resigned myself to "It's going to take a long time," and settled down for the long haul.

On August 9th, 2013, five months after our file was submitted to China, it happened. It was a Friday, and Fridays were busy for me. I volunteered in Sarah Kate's class in the morning, then taught back-to-back classes of second graders for Religious Education at the kids' school, then rushed home to have ten minutes of down time before my Bible study group arrived at my house. I was printing out my talking points for that day's discussion when my eye caught a page of notes in Brian's handwriting. It said something like, "girl . . . eleven months . . . Lianjiang . . . shared list . . . forty-eight hours."

My hands started shaking. My mouth went dry. What?? *What?!* I immediately called Brian and sputtered, "*Did you forget to tell me something?*" Meaning, "Seriously, did that call that we've been waiting months for finally come, and I wasn't here, and you just jotted down some notes for me to find off-handedly, and didn't think to *let me in on the news?*"

He explained that our social worker called while I was teaching at the school, so he knew he couldn't reach me. I got more details. We had been matched with an eleven-month-old baby named Yonghui, and had forty-eight hours to review her file and say yes or no. *Let's not forget my inability to make quick decisions.*

Brian forwarded me the file our social worker had sent, and all of a sudden, there she was. That face. Beautiful. Big eyes, chubby cheeks (like all our kids!). There she was.

I had always imagined the day that we found out who our little girl was would be one of the happiest, most exciting days of my life—that I would be overcome with joy and excitement, bursting at the seams. What did I feel instead? Heaviness. Fear. Grief.

I expected joy. What I didn't anticipate was to grieve the loss of what was currently Our Family. We had a good thing going. The children were ten, eight, and six, and, while parenting is never a cake-walk, I reckon these ages are pretty close to being perfect. The oldest hadn't become sassy, and the youngest was physically independent. On Saturdays, I could sleep in because my kids tiptoed down the hallway, zapped a breakfast pastry, and popped in their own DVD. (What can I say? Parenting diligence goes out the window with the opportunity to sleep past six a.m.) They can put themselves to bed if need be. They can all read. They can entertain themselves. They're all in school. I repeat, *they are all in school!*

More than that, they are great kids. They are bright and funny and thoughtful and creative. They each do really well in school, and, besides one child's occasional smart remarks, they get glowing behavior reports from their teachers. They're not without their challenges, but overall, they are well-adjusted, awesome kids. Why would I mess this up?

Not only was I grieving the loss of our current family dynamics, I was anticipating the loss of my life as I knew it. All three kids being in school brought me freedom and time to work, to do ministry, and to be involved in the community. Most of my friends have school-aged kids, and we could meet for coffee dates. I got to grocery shop every week *by myself!*

So, I'm looking at this petite face on the computer screen, and there is part of me that screams, "What have I done?" I know nothing about this little person, other than a few pictures and measurements and limited medical history. She may have more extensive special needs than her file indicates. She may really struggle academically. She may have attachment issues, behavioral issues, speech issues, growth issues. She may demand more of me than I have to give.

What about going back to the baby days? When we told our agency we were willing to take a child three or younger, we really expected to get a three-year-old, because we were willing to take a three-year-old. We were totally floored to be matched with a *baby!* We would be back to diapers, teething, potty training, and sleepless nights.

What about the age gap? I imagined a three-year age gap between her and Sarah Kate, and now we had a five-year difference. The picture I had in my head of the girls playing dolls together dissipated. I remember putting Sarah Kate to bed that night and literally feeling like someone was standing on my chest. I felt so heavy, so tired, so overwhelmed, and so fearful that we were about to "mess up our family." Then I felt such guilt that I felt this way on what should have been one of the happiest days of our lives.

I wrestled with God about this sadness, wondering if this meant she wasn't the one, or that we were not meant to adopt after all. God reminded me of part of a sermon by a friend, which He previously used to confirm we were supposed to walk this adoption road: "*We're often attracted to the easy thing, but at the end there is no joy or reward. Often, the right thing is the costly thing, but infinitely worth it.*"

My grief was not a red flag indicating that we were making a mistake; instead, it was a sign I was counting the cost one more time. It's one thing to talk adoption and imagine the cute multi-racial family photos and fantasize about what a beautiful thing it will be. It's another matter to stare into strange, expressionless eyes that have never known love, and to say, "Yes, I will be your mother. I will lay down my rights and my ease and my security and take you as my own, no matter what trials or sufferings you bring with you. You will be mine."

God did a miracle. In those forty-eight hours, He allowed me to walk through my emotions, lay down life as I knew it, and embrace with joy this precious little girl, whom we would call Lucy Mei. Brian and I watched her videos over and over, and we laughed with delight when she cocked her head and looked straight into the camera. We said, "That's our girl!"

She became worth it—totally and completely worth it. We chose to say "yes," and, in our hearts, she became ours.

Even though she would not *officially* be ours for another few months, we added her into our "new normal." Her birthday was September 17th, so we had a family birthday party for her. Unfortunately, my dreams of authentic Chinese clothing, a stunning cake, and a perfect photo to add to her Adoption Memory Book did not quite flesh out as I thought. First of all, I convinced Andrew that his Chinese dress was not a girls' outfit, but it totally was. Secondly, my Double Decker Oreo Cream Cake was such a disaster that it looked like it fell on the floor and had been scooped up and slopped onto a fancy dish. I can see Lucy flipping through her baby book years from now saying, "Really? This is the best you could do?" I'm pretty sure the orphanage could have come up with something better for her. I hate you, Pinterest.

Birthday parties aside, the talk around our house became all about bunk beds and shared spaces and making room in our house and hearts for one more. We could not have been happier. Did I still get fearful and wonder if we were doing the right thing? Did I still feel anxious? Absolutely. Yet, instead of seeing my emotions as a warning light that we should abort All Things Hard, they became a sweet reminder that God's goal for my life is not my comfort and ease. Hardships, discomfort are extensions of His tender mercy because He uses them to whittle away the countless idols to which I vainly cling.

Chapter 5

I'm Dreaming of a Guangzhou Christmas

The four months between the day we were matched with Lucy and the day she became ours was quite possibly the most difficult period of the whole journey. Instead of pursuing the idea of a child, we were now pursuing an actual baby with a name and an adorable face. The orphanage had named her Yonghui Lian; we would call her Lucy Mei. We could picture her alone in her crib, isolated from care and affection, and we grieved that we could not speed up the process to get to her. We prepared the best ways we knew, not knowing exactly when the boxes would all be checked, clearing us for travel.

Despite the uncertainty of our departure date, my thoughtful, proactive friend Stacey decided I needed a baby shower. It had been five years since we had a baby in the house, so we were starting all over in the baby gear department. Still, I must say that preparing for your fourth baby is quite different than getting ready for your first. When I was pregnant with Joshua, Brian endured hours of strolling up and down the aisles of Babies R Us, hand-in-hand with a hormonally irrational wife. I belabored stroller options, bathtub safety, and color coordinating. Stealing an idea from the latest Pottery Barn Kids catalog, I had the poor man paint blue stripes on the nursery walls, which were required to be perfectly straight and equidistant. I'll pause here to let you mull over how long that task took my incredibly patient husband. Let's not skip the fact that when we moved two years later, I had him paint the blue stripes *again*. I'm evil, I know.

The fourth time around, if someone said, "Hey, I have a such-and-such I'm not using anymore, do you want it?" I replied, "Absolutely!" Color and brand became irrelevant. Most of the time I thought, "Huh. I forgot that when you had a baby you needed a (stroller, Baby Bjorn, diaper bag, etc.)."

As you can tell, my mental state was not the sharpest at this stage, so I was grateful Stacey took the initiative to help us stock up on supplies. But let me tell you, you have never been to a baby shower even remotely like this one.

Seriously, never.

I should have been suspicious when Stacey was peculiarly vague about the details of the event. "What time is the shower?" Stacey: "Ummm, be ready around eight in the morning, maybe?" Weird, but okay. "What should I wear?" "Dress comfortably." Since when is a party dress comfortable? I should have known that with Stacey, my friend who likes to "think outside the square," as the Aussies say, this would be no ordinary party.

The morning of the shower, I awoke at my usual time, 4:15 a.m., because Queensland does not believe in daylight savings time, and in the summer, this is when the sun and birds rise. I am never happy about this fact. I dozed on and off, and began to hear some commotion around 6:15. I never could have anticipated the situation that was coming down my hallway. Before I knew what was happening, I was kidnapped by a ninja, a gorilla and a ghost, aka, suburban housewives who raided their kids' dress up boxes and were *way* too enthusiastically aggressive for a ridiculously early Saturday morning. What in the world?

They kindly instructed me to change into shorts and a tank top, but there was no time for make-up. Right. "So, we *will* come back here so I can change into my party dress before the actual shower, right guys?" No response. When we got to the car, they ditched their costumes and gave me one of my own for the car ride—a Transformer mask, so I wouldn't know where we were going. This precaution was completely unnecessary, as I have no sense of direction even without a mask on, but I let them have their fun.

We finally arrived at our destination, and my captors exchanged my mask for a hideous gorilla head, which they made me wear as we walked on what felt like gravel for about fifteen minutes. You're welcome, joggers, for providing you with a hilarious topic of conversation for your post-jog coffee dates.

I finally got to ditch the mask and take in my surroundings—a hiking trail on scenic Mt. Coot-tha, and a group of my dear friends. They handed me a written description of what was about to take place: "a journey filled with ups and downs, potential frustrations, but definite rewards, much like this adoption journey." This trip would not be an ordinary hike to the top; instead, it would be a Pilgrim's Progress voyage of sorts, with presents hidden along the way. A box of baby snacks was secreted in a bush, with a verse about Jesus being our source of nourishment. A packet of wipes perched on the top of a post, with an accompanying note about Jesus washing us white as snow. I discovered treasures throughout the upward hike, until we finally reached our destination—the mountain top café, where more friends were waiting to join us for breakfast. (*Note: All of these friends were wearing party dresses/something really cute and make-up. They, unlike I, were not the least bit sweaty. This contrast made for some interesting pictures. "Who's the one having the baby?" observers asked. "Oh, the non-pregnant one in the stained tank top with the pillow creases on her face."*)

Despite the unconventional nature of the day, I cannot express how much I loved that baby shower for so many different reasons.

First of all, I felt known. Laughter is my favorite, so kidnappings and practical jokes and gorilla masks speak my love language. It was also unbelievably thoughtful. Especially in a culture where adoption is so rare, my friends knew that a traditional baby shower might have felt awkward. The fact that we did something completely crazy and non-traditional took away any potential unease on my part or those people in attendance.

Friends in Halloween costumes + hiking in a gorilla mask + inspirational yet practical gifts + ricotta pancakes = Best. Baby Shower. Ever. I dare you to try to top it.

My friends stocked me with baby essentials just in time, because within a few days, we received the long-awaited news of our departure date. Our entire family was set to fly to Guangzhou on Saturday, December 14th, and our "Gotcha Day," when Lucy would be placed in our arms, would be Monday the 16th. It was really happening! Even though we knew this day would come, it still felt so surreal. The hugeness of it all sent me into a manic frenzy.

I have never been great at seeing an enormous task and calmly breaking it down into smaller, more manageable steps. Instead, I just see the enormity of it all and either temporarily become ADHD, or completely shut down. I oscillated between the two of these extremes hourly in those last few days before our departure.

My conversations with Brian went something like: "Well, if our flight leaves, because we need some prescriptions, I think Lucy wears a size 12 months. What is congee?" Makes total sense, right? Brian's reaction: "I cannot handle you in this state."

One day, I looked at my mile-long to-do list, and said, "Right. It looks like the best thing for me to do right now is to go to Kmart and print out Sarah Kate's Disney princess pictures that have sat in our computer for the last six months." Don't even try to follow my logic.

Shut down looks like this: Me sobbing in my bed, in the fetal position. "It's too mu-u-u-u-u-uch!!" My mom heard this sob-speech at the end of every semester of college. Pretty sure she just put the phone down and pushed play on a pre-recorded response of "You can do it. Take one thing at a time. You will get through."

Despite my unstable mental state, the tasks were completed one by one, and we pondered for the millionth time how life was about to change. Life as we knew it would never be the same. Our six year old, Sarah Kate, wrote a few entries in her journal about her anticipation of a new sister:

> *My family is adopting a little girl from China. We have done every step except getting her. I am very excited because we are leaving for China tomorrow. I can't wait. When I see my little sister Lucy I will hug her very, very gently because she is very little. When Lucy gets a bit bigger I will tell her about Christmas and what Christmas is all about. I am not going to do anything that will hurt her because she is very little and that would not be loving. I love Lucy very much even though I haven't seen her in real life before.*

Precious. But this next entry is the one that got to me the most: *(This is exactly how she wrote it; I've just corrected her spelling.)*

Introduction:

My Dad bought a new dresser yesterday. I am now putting things on it.

Problem:

But I will have a little sister and I have to share it with her, so she has to put things on it too. So, it might be a mess.

Conclusion:

That doesn't matter.

That's it, isn't it? Lucy's anticipated arrival had already caused frenzy, excitement, and "my-life-is-turning-upside-down" fear. When the time came for her to join our family, our neat little lives would become very, very messy. **But that doesn't matter** because if life is merely a series of efforts to avoid messiness, to avoid heartache, unease, and suffering, it is a sad, hollow life indeed.

Yet, how often do we make decisions out of a desire to avoid a mess? We pursue friendships with people who will cause the least amount of pain. We spend our money on what will bring the most pleasure and the least risk. Our greatest desires for our lives are reflected in our Facebook posts: our gorgeous, glossy children running happily through fields of clover, while we and our spouses, dressed in our Sunday best and not a hair out of place, look on with pride and joy. We say, "Look at me! This is my life!" and we order our days in such a way as to try to make the pictures true.

If happy and glossy and perfect are all that we are striving towards to call this a life well lived, we've missed out on life's greatest riches.

My six year old got that. *She got it.* "*It might be a mess, but that doesn't matter*" because the most beautiful things in life are created through struggle and hardship. The greatest joys are birthed through tears. A tiny fifteen-month-old life in Lianjiang is a life worth saving, regardless of the tornado of distress and discomfort she might possibly bring with her. It might be a mess. That doesn't matter. Before our journey to Lucy was done, the truth of these words would be tested to the fullest extent.

Chapter 6

I Think They Got Us Confused With Brangelina

I have a crazy recommendation. Celebrate Christmas two weeks early. Try it. I dare you.

We were forced into this situation because of our December 14th departure date. We would be in China on Christmas Day, and we certainly weren't lugging presents and stockings all the way to Guangzhou, so we declared December 8th Christmas Day at the Phillips' house. Why not?

The night before, we totally pretended like it was Christmas Eve. We played Christmas music and ate Christmas cookies and watched a Christmas movie, then turned out the lights and read the Christmas story by candlelight. Then, time for bed, kids! Tomorrow is Christmas!

"But how will Santa know—"

(Me interrupting) "Who wants more Christmas cookies?"

(*Note: Brian and I never could make up our minds about whether or not we would "do Santa," so when the kids were born, we didn't "do" Santa, but we didn't "not do Santa" either. Weird, I know. This indecision has left my kids in a Christmas conundrum that I'm sure will be sorted out by a psychologist one day.*)

Everyone was up at the crack of dawn the next day—more because of the blazing 4:30 a.m. sunrise than excitement—and happy children yelled, "It's Christmas!" The neighborhood kids were confused.

We ate homemade cinnamon rolls (because there ain't no Pillsbury down here in Australia) and tore through presents one by one. We did every single Christmas tradition we usually do, just two weeks early. In a way, it didn't really matter, because our Christmas traditions have changed so much since moving to Brisbane, where Christmas is crazy hot.

I don't think I'll ever get used to sweating in December. Our first Christmas here, I was *bit-ter*. Our house, like most Aussie houses, does not have central air conditioning, and it was one hundred and five degrees the week of Christmas—105. Now, sure, I could look on the bright side and say, "Oh wow! We get to swim on Christmas Day! Isn't that awesome, kids? I mean, who gets to do that?" But let's be honest. For a nostalgic traditionalist like me, a hot Christmas just ISN'T RIGHT.

To me, a summertime Christmas is bizarre. Shopping malls blare "Let it Snow" while their patrons walk around in tank tops and flip flops. You can actually buy a giant inflatable Frosty the Snowman if you so choose. Shops sell t-shirts with snowflakes on them. As a native northern hemispherian, I implore you: Why, pray tell, would they do this if *deep down* they didn't think that a hot Christmas is inherently wrong? It isn't natural, I tell you.

Besides the heat, it took me a while to get used to the Christmas décor, or lack thereof. One of my favorite Christmas traditions in America was driving through neighborhoods and looking at Christmas lights. Here, you might get one house per suburb that put forth an effort. You know why they don't decorate as much? Because it's TOO HOT! Who wants to string lights and suffer a heat stroke? I get it. It's not worth it.

That first year, I couldn't even decorate my own house well because our MAIL ORDER CHRISTMAS TREE that we purchased in October did not arrive until the week of Christmas. Despite years of tradition, we couldn't have a live tree because (a) They don't grow here, and (b) It wouldn't last two days because it is, all together now, TOO BLAZING HOT. I half expected our tree, when it was finally delivered, to arrive in a puddle of melted green goo. If that doesn't scream Happy Holidays, I don't know what does.

Regardless, this year, our new Australian summertime Christmas traditions were finished by December 9th. Can I tell you what was awesome about that? By December 9th we were *done with Christmas.* Now, that may make some of you nostalgic types sad, but let's unpack the idea, shall we? Christmas shopping? Done. Baking? Done. Christmas parties? Done. Pressure to put on the best Christmas ever? Done, done, done. Then I could gloatingly gaze at everyone else rushing around in Pinterest-induced mania and shout, "Suckas!" Ah, what a feeling.

So, Christmas was "done and dusted," to quote an Aussie phrase, and the countdown quickly wound down to zero. The day was finally here. After a year and a half of paperwork, dreaming, and preparing, our departure day finally arrived. It was time to go get our girl.

I'm pretty sure someone with the authority to make things happen got our family confused with Brangelina (easy mistake to make), because from the moment our journey began, we were given the superstar treatment. If we had known what was about to happen after we got to the USA, we might not have enjoyed it so much, but ignorance is bliss, right?

Our royal status began when we checked in for our flight. The airline worker asked why we were going to China, so we told her about our adoption. She was pumped. When it came time to assign seats, she coyly said, "Oh, it looks like you booked into Premium seating." Brian answered, "Don't we wish!" To which she replied, "No, you're nice people. You're in Premium." To which we replied, "Thank you very much!"

The flight was awesome, especially since we were coming from Australia, making the flight a mere nine hours, and the time difference only three. Our kids are used to grueling twenty-six hour travel times to America, so to them this flight was a piece of cake. Three movies back to back, a little reading, a lot of snacks, and boom, we were there!

Our province guide met us at the Guangzhou airport and accompanied us to the Garden Hotel, a stunningly beautiful establishment where many adoptive families stay. At the hotel we were met with more good news. Due to an overbooking, the hotel upgraded us to a three-bedroom, three-bath suite! We couldn't believe it.

The best part about the upgrade, according to my kids? The toilets, or as Andrew deemed them, the ABWs—"Automatic Bum Warmers." A quick glance at the *control panel* on the side of the toilet revealed anything you could ever want in a toilet, but never knew was possible. Seat warmers, rear cleansing, soft rear cleansing for you sensitive types, power deodorizing (I don't even want to know what that is), drying, and the list goes on. Joshua actually declared: "I could sit on that toilet for hours!" Things I also heard in reference to the fancy potties: Andrew: "Hey Joshua, let's go wash and dry our bums!" (They immediately sprint down the hall.) Anytime I heard someone cackling like a minion, I knew a kid was in the bathroom. Guangzhou who? The kids didn't need sightseeing; they were completely entertained by the ridiculous toilets!

The hotel even gave Brian a celebrity-style birthday. After getting a Grammy-worthy rendition of Happy Birthday at the Banana Leaf Restaurant by a group of Chinese guitar players who obviously wished they had a different job, we returned from dinner and the doorbell—yes, the doorbell—rang. A nice gentleman delivered a pure chocolate cake in the shape of a present that was to die for. How did they know? They just knew. *They knew.*

Despite the rock star treatment, the best part of our accommodation was *the simple wooden crib* beside our bed. I couldn't stop staring at it. That was where *she* would sleep, in less than twenty-four hours. The one we'd waited for, prayed for, loved from afar for so long. She would no longer be a photo on our fridge; instead, she would be here, in the flesh, asleep beside us as ours. It was all becoming very real. We were not on vacation. We were in China to gain a forever child.

December 15th, 2013

Tonight is her last night in the orphanage. Her last night to sleep in a room with dozens of other babies. Her last night to be put to bed without a snuggle and a bedtime story. Her last night to wake up cold or wet or hungry and have no one there to meet her needs. Her last night without a family.

And you know what? She has no idea.

Isn't it fitting that Lucy should arrive at Christmas? For almost two years, we have pursued, labored, poured out much expense and prayers to bring this little girl home, and she has no idea. She isn't asking for us to come. She does not even know who we are. But soon we will arrive and turn her little life upside down, for the good.

And when we weren't looking for Him, when we were far off, when we didn't even know who He was, God pursued us by sending His Son Jesus, to turn our lives upside down—for the good. This Christmas we get to go to China to meet our little baby and bring her home. I am so thankful that two thousand years ago God came to us as a little baby, so that one day we can all go home.

This little girl that we have hoped for—she may initially reject us. She may fight our love out of fear. She may cry and grieve. Yet we will love her fiercely. She will bring nothing with her except the worn clothes on her back, yet we desire to give her the world. She does not have to do a thing to earn or deserve our love. We have chosen to love her, no matter what.

Because isn't that the way that God loves us?

I sit here, hours before we hold our daughter for the very first time, and I'm a jumble of emotions. My heart is nostalgic, as I know that I kissed my kids goodnight for the very last time as a mother of three. For my sake more than theirs, I reassured them again that my love for them would never change, no matter how many people are in our family. I grieved as I sang Sarah Kate to sleep for the very last time as my baby, my youngest, my only girl.

Yet my heart is full, because I know that tomorrow, God is carrying to completion what He began in our hearts so many years ago. So, whatever tomorrow holds, I'm in. And I just can't wait.

Chapter 7

Orphan No More

December 16th, 2013—Gotcha Day.

I'm not sure how I feel about the term "Gotcha Day." It is such a casual phrase for a cataclysmic, universe-altering, yet intensely intimate event. I mean, if you're playing tag in the yard, or if you squish a fly, or if you finally find that kid who somehow wedged himself on the upper shelf of the linen closet behind stacks of folded towels in an epic game of hide and seek, then sure, "Gotcha" is completely appropriate. But to place that label on the day when a child you did not birth is placed in your arms and called your own? Not sure that's the best phrase we could come up with.

Odd name or not, this was THE DAY. The main event. No turning back. Excitement was high as we got ready that morning. We tried to act normal, but who were we fooling? With every tooth brushed, every button buttoned, every hair tucked carefully in place, our thoughts were all the same: Oh my word. Today she will be ours. We ate our last meals as a family of five, and nervously bided our time until the van arrived mid-afternoon to take us to the Civil Affairs building. It was game time.

Now, all the training we received beforehand told us to have low expectations for Gotcha Day. "It's not ceremonious at all," they said. "The child is simply brought out and handed to you, no fanfare." We knew Lucy would probably be upset, as she would be handed over to weird-looking strangers who talked funny. There would be no warm atmosphere or dramatic music playing in the background. Instead, the "delivery" would take place in a sterile government building with a dozen other families receiving crying, traumatized children. There would be nothing glamorous about this moment, and we were prepared for it.

I was also ready for the possibilities of how I might feel when I held her for the first time. There is nothing natural about adoption, and attachment is a process for the family and the child. I was prepared to feel initially like someone else's child was being placed in my arms, and that was okay. We would get there. Clinically prepared for adoption to take place? Check.

The moment arrived. Our guide said, "She's here," and an agent announced, "Lian Yonghui." We rounded the corner, and out walked a Chinese caretaker cradling an infant—our baby.

That moment is so hard to put into words. I literally felt like time stood still as Yonghui, Lucy, was gently placed in my embrace. Something absolutely supernatural happened in those next few moments. I took her all in—her layers upon layers of clothing, her deep, big eyes staring warily at me, her chubby cheeks, her fingers the size of a newborn's, and I knew. I knew she was mine. Watching the video later, I was amazed to see my expression was the same look of elation and love that was on my face the first time my other three were placed on my chest in the hospital. It was the look of a new mother completely, head-over-heels in love with her child.

God did that.

Throughout the adoption process, I questioned our decision, as I do all major decisions in my life. (Ah, the blessings and curses of being analytical.) One night I broke down and asked Brian, "Do I only want to adopt because I want Sarah Kate to have a little sister? Because that's not a good enough reason. What if I decided to adopt because I'm so dramatic, and I like good stories? *Please tell me we're not adopting a child because I think it will make a great story! Because that is a terrible reason to turn our family upside down."* Thankfully, he assured me repeatedly that those things weren't true, but still, how could I know that we were doing the right thing?

My answer came in the way my heart leapt at the mere sight of her. Doubts dissipated and God's plan became crystal clear when from first sight, I knew I would die for her. She wasn't a stranger; she was simply mine. There is a scene in the movie *Hook* in which one of the Lost Boys feels and stretches Robin Williams' aged face, then gasps in recognition, "Oh there you are Peter!" When I contemplated my new daughter in all her beauty, I felt like saying, "Oh there you are Lucy! You've been missing from our family, and for so long we didn't even know it. You're not a stranger. I see you now, and I love you."

I know this reaction is not the case for many adoptive mamas, as they struggle for what feels like a very long time to feel genuine affection towards their adopted child. Attachment is not usually instantaneous. Maybe the Lord knew that my analytical self needed an extra dose of assurance this day.

Brian and the kids gently loved on Lucy as she alternated between stunned silence and short, quiet sobs. Who could blame her? It was all too much, and within minutes, she was fast asleep.

The drive back to the hotel was so surreal. We rode with another adoptive family who, like us, within a span of twenty minutes in a Civil Affairs building, gained a child. We drove to a building together, and drove back with two new babies. Beautifully bizarre.

Lucy awoke when we got back to the hotel, and boy, was she not happy. Again, who could blame her? From the perspective of the child, international adoption is comparable to an alien abduction. She had been taken from everything familiar and thrust into new sights, smells, and sensations. For a child who was used to isolation most hours of the day, this was an overwhelming case of sensory overload.

We spent the next three hours playing, "What will help Lucy to stop crying?" This involved bubbles, blocks, bottles, Chinese lullabies sung by Jackie Chan, and whatever would work. She was most entertained, if by entertained you mean not crying, by a balloon that she tapped over and over with the backs of her fingers, so Brian and I took turns holding her and that sacred balloon.

We didn't mind.

Lucy was worn out by the enormity of the day, and more than happy for bedtime to arrive. Tears filled my eyes as I rocked her and sang, "Amazing Grace, how sweet the sound, that saved a wretch like me." What an amazing privilege to hold a physical representation of the gospel. What an honor to call this precious one daughter, and, for the first time in her life, to lead her lovingly into rest with lullabies and tender kisses and whispers of love. "You are safe. You are mine." Her eyes grew heavy, and she slept.

When Lucy awoke twelve hours later (yes, she slept all night!), she was happy, until she saw our faces. I think reality set in for her that we were here to stay, and we would actually be all up in her business. The crying began, and continued for the next several days. Triggers for the crying included but were not limited to sitting down, standing up, touching her face, getting too close, trying to feed her anything but a bottle, and loud mouth noises like smacking. (Okay, not really that one, but it is one of my personal pet peeves and makes me want to cry.)

You know it's bad when a bus full of other adoptive families walking through their own traumatic transitions are looking at you like, "You poor thing." Yep. We were that family. Even her body language screamed rejection. When we held her, Lucy would literally do a back bend to get as far away from us as possible.

Sarah Kate's travel journal entry said it all:

Dear Lucy,
I hope you grow up to love Mommy and Daddy and not push them away. I love you. You are as cute as a butterfly. You are also as cute as a baby that was just born, but you were not just born. Did you know that your eyelashes are almost as long as

mine? I think you are cuter than I was when I was a baby. Do
you know why you cry all the time? (Here she put a long line for
Lucy to fill in the blank. If only it were that easy!) *Lucy, did*
you know I have a shirt that says "Cute as a Button" on it? I want
it to belong to you when it is too small for me. Love, Sarah Kate

We knew there was the possibility she would reject us, but it
didn't make it any easier when it actually happened. The reasons for
her rejection broke our hearts.

December 18, 2013

The past few days, we've been on Cry Patrol. I'm not going to
lie. Lucy cries. A lot. And like I've said before, I don't blame her.
    What breaks my heart is that the place where she's most
content is by herself, in her crib, on her back. This is how she
probably spent most hours of her days in the orphanage. She can
be screaming her head off, but if I lay her in the bed and walk
away, she's immediately quiet. Her hands are her playmates,
as they have been all her life, because that's all she had to play
with in her crib for hours on end. She taps them on her head,
claps them together, and wraps her fingers around each other.
She rocks her head back and forth in a self-soothing way. This
is where she feels safe, because this is what's familiar. It's what
she knows.
    We want to kiss her and play with her, but these things,
for the most part, are terrifying to her. It reminds me of one of
my favorite C.S. Lewis quotes from Mere Christianity: *"Our*
desires are not too strong, but too weak. We are half-hearted
creatures, fooling about with drink and sex and ambition when
infinite joy is offered us, like an ignorant child who wants to
go on making mud pies in a slum because he cannot imagine

what is meant by the offer of a holiday at the sea. We are far too easily pleased."

Just like we are so often satisfied with pleasures that are fleeting and weak in comparison with the satisfaction and peace that God offers us through a relationship with Him, Lucy is not only content with, but prefers playing with her hands in a dark room, flat on her back, because she can't even imagine that our love is better.

Then we see glimpses of hope. Her tentative hand reaches out and touches my face. She leans in when I pick her up instead of throwing herself backwards. She smiles when I greet her in the morning instead of screaming with fright.

These moments only happen a few times each day, but we'll take them because they are glimpses of what Lucy will one day be when she knows us, trusts us, and believes that we love her extravagantly.

So for now, sweet Lucy, sleep well. We'll give you space, we'll respect all that you've been through so far in your short little life, and we'll celebrate the baby steps that will one day cause you to run joyfully and willingly into our loving arms.

Chapter 8

Bye-Bye Parenting Books

"I'm going to have a special needs child one day."

I heard it clear as day. I was in high school, at church on a Sunday night as usual, and someone was sharing from the pulpit about his own special needs child, and the challenges and blessings that come with this unique form of parenting. All other details of the night are fuzzy, but I remember being overwhelmed by the thought that one day, that special needs parent would be me.

As a teenage girl, this idea terrified me and I dismissed the thought. When I grew up, got married, and started having babies, each pregnancy triggered my mind to revisit that night and I wondered, would this be the one? After my third and (so I thought) last child received a clean bill of health, I was sure I had "dodged the bullet," so to speak.

If only I knew then that basing my dreams for my children on the degree of their physical health, and my subsequent ease, created pitifully small dreams. There is no way I could have known that five years after we declared the childbearing years officially over and called it a healthy family of five, not only would God give me a special needs child, but He also would have so transformed my heart that I would purposefully pursue this child at great cost.

Still, the decision was a frightening one. We were choosing to prefer a child who fit the category of "something is wrong," and that "something" could be much more extensive than the child's limited medical file revealed. This condition was definitely the case with Lucy.

The more time we spent with her, the more we were aware of Lucy's developmental challenges. Before packing our bags for China, I polled other moms who had adopted kids around Lucy's age, and a common theme in advice was: "Pack the right snacks (yogurt melts) and toys (rattles, dolls), and you'll win her over for sure." So that's what I did. The problem was, we quickly discovered that Lucy had never had anything in her mouth besides a bottle, and she couldn't grasp things, due to lack of motor skills, weakness, and sensory issues. So, she wouldn't eat the yogurt melts that apparently are always a home run, or anything else for that matter. She only stared blankly at the toys. Obviously, she wasn't ready for the shape sorter I packed. Perfect. We were left to woo her with our irresistible charm and wit.

Honestly, we were shocked by Lucy's teensy size and the extent of her developmental delays. At fifteen months, she was the size of a small six month old, and was developmentally like a five month old. We quickly had to get used to the concerned looks on people's faces when they found out how old she was. "Yes, she's fifteen months. Yes, I know she looks like an infant. No, she isn't walking."

Not only was she not walking, but she also couldn't roll over, sit unsupported, crawl, or pick up toys. She screamed if we even came close with a spoon or any form of food. She was terrified of it. This problem caused the otherwise amazing breakfast buffet at our hotel to be not so amazing. She would cry the entire meal. Eating outside the hotel was an even more delightful experience. Let's just say no one was knocking down our door asking to be dinner buddies. Poor Lucy. Fifteen months of lying on her back with little stimulation and only a bottle for nourishment had taken its toll.

Lucy was smaller and farther behind than her file stated. Yet, just as we readily accepted whatever challenges came with our biological children, we felt the same about Lucy. If she always remained behind, she was ours. If she always stayed extremely small, she was ours. If she never overcame her sensory disorders, she was ours. We weren't really scared anymore; we just wanted to care for her in the best possible way. This meant re-thinking milestones, measures of success, expectations, and pretty much every other parenting philosophy or technique we used with our other three.

Lucy is on a bottle at fifteen months? If she needs that bottle for fifteen more months to feel secure, that's perfectly fine. (I'm pretty sure I was getting paid back for all the judgmental looks I've shot three year olds chugging a bottle or sucking a pacifier like it's their job.) She won't eat solid foods? Let's go super slow and work to desensitize that mouth so that food doesn't feel like sandpaper anymore. This may take months. She will put up a fight. That's okay. Not sitting or crawling? We'll give her lots of tummy time and redeem the months she missed out on strengthening those core muscles.

We were committed to letting her progress through all those steps she'd missed, on her own timetable, and if it took six months or more before she walked, so be it. Former rigid positions on eating, sleeping, waking, bonding, and schedules? Forget about it. Out the window. Adios. You're not welcome here anymore. Not with this kid.

This position was not easy for a control freak like me, but it was necessary and freeing.

December 21, 2013

Well, it seems as if even our spacious three-bedroom apartment isn't big enough to prevent germ sharing. We've all come down with colds. I don't know if it's cold medicine fog or just being ready to go home, but we're definitely in the throes of delirium. Here are a few examples:

- *We ate KFC last night and thought it was delicious. "Look guys! They even put gravy on this itty bitty container of mashed potatoes!"*
- *After staring into space for quite some time, Andrew says, "Mom, what if you had named me Ralph? I mean, think about how different my life would be if my name was actually Ralph!"*
- *Today I danced with Lucy in our living room to the sweet, soothing voice of Jackie Chan.*
- *Lucy stopped crying when I sang, so I serenaded her for quite some time. I actually ran out of songs and started singing the word "music" over and over again. She liked it, so I sang the word "music" for fifteen minutes straight. "Music, music, music, music, music, music." (Did you know that if you say the word "music" over and over again, it doesn't sound like a real word anymore? Try it.)*
- *I was explaining a medical condition to Brian that has a side effect of incontinence. He said, "Oh sad, they can't have babies?"*

Yep. We've got a case of the Crazies.

Yesterday was Medical Appointment Day. Lordy, lordy.

While Brian and the boys stayed behind, Lucy and I, along with two other families, loaded up in the van and went to the medical center for a required check-up. First came the picture taking (not really sure what this was for). Picture taking for the other two families looked like this: The moms carried their calm little two-year-old girls one by one into the photo room. They sat quietly in front of the camera, and were done in thirty seconds max combined. At this moment, I did not struggle with comparison or envy in the least bit (I just lied).

Nobody puts Lucy in a corner. Nobody. So, she screamed, and screamed. Our guide and I had to hold her to get her even semi-photographable. The miracle photographer caught her between screams as she was taking a breath, so the picture actually looks like she's smiling. Amazing.

Then came the actual medical examination. She loved this just as much as getting her picture taken. Bless her. Thankfully, because she's under the age of two, she didn't require any shots. I cannot even imagine how that would have gone.

That was yesterday. Today, however, we had a huge breakthrough. While some Guangzhou friends took Brian and the older kids on a sightseeing frenzy, Lucy and I headed back to the room for a Girls' Day In. I'll be honest. I wasn't feeling well, so I was really looking forward to taking a nap when Lucy did. If there's one thing Lucy has been a champ at since we got her, it's sleeping. We lay her down and she goes right to sleep without a fuss. Except for today.

I laid her down, and she started crying. What is this? I checked on her, started to walk away, and she started crying again. Beg your pardon? The baby who only wants to be left alone? This happened about six times. I comforted her, she calmed down, but as soon as I walked away she started crying again. I was overjoyed!

Now you have to understand my perspective. I'm the Baby-Wise Mom, the Queen of Tough Love. I readily let my other three cry it out, because, dadgum it, they were going to learn to put themselves to sleep so I wasn't rocking myself straight into Crazy Town for hours every night. But Lucy has had fifteen months of putting herself to sleep. I've seen her do it. She taps her head with the back of her fingers and rolls her head back and forth. These have been her lullabies.

This time she cried because she wanted me there. She cried because she knew I'd come. I couldn't believe it! Is she really starting to understand?

With this baby, there will be no crying it out, because I want her to know that she now has someone who will come when she cries, no matter what. You'd better believe I gladly scooped her up! It was such a joy, just like it is a privilege to change her diaper immediately when she's wet, or rush to her aid when she cries out in the night. These are things I took for granted, and at times found laborious and mundane with my other three, but I take delight in them with Lucy. I feel like each time I immediately meet her need, God is redeeming the isolation and neglect that she experienced all those months.

I eventually got that much-needed nap, but this time, it was with Lucy asleep in my arms like she's belonged there all along—because she has.

Such a turning point for us. In a way, we both experienced small victories that day. I was able to release my need to go by the book, and she began to loosen her grip on an unhealthy independence that resulted from extensive isolation to which no infant should be subjected. We both let go and stepped toward each other. She said, "I need you." I said, "I'm here, right away, even if it's inconvenient." It was beautiful. She was needy, and that was a very good thing.

As for the rest of her "special needs"? Potential attachment disorders, sensory disorders, developmental delays, nowhere near the growth curve? Yes, Lucy has special needs, but don't we all? We're all uniquely created in the image of God, and He looks at each of us, with our own phobias and weaknesses of all kinds, and He sees our flaws, hidden and obvious. He sees where we just can't keep up with the others. He knows that we feel delayed, lesser than. Yet, He says, "You are mine. It is a good thing to be needy. Your flaws create space for me to rush in and scoop you up and hold you to My chest, like you've belonged there all along, because you have."

We would be wise to snuggle up.

Chapter 9

Miles to Go Before I Sleep

Our time in China came to a close almost as quickly as it began. We signed documents promising to never abandon or abuse Lucy, and we promised to love her well. We gave her our name, and she was no longer Yonghui Lian—a name assigned to her based on the name of her orphanage. She was Lucy Mei Phillips, our "beautiful light."

After a ten-day whirlwind of paperwork, sightseeing, and crying (mostly Lucy, sometimes Brian and me), it was time to go. We said our good-byes to our beloved guides and to the other American families who walked those ten days with us, and prepared for the inevitable family separation that would begin at the Guangzhou airport.

We were all dreading this departure. Brian and our three older children were headed to one terminal, Australia-bound. Lucy and I were boarding a plane for America. We knew from the beginning of the adoption process that Lucy would have to land on American soil to obtain U.S. citizenship. We could not afford for our entire family to go to China, then to America. The logical solution was for Lucy and me to spend two weeks in the States getting her citizenship and U.S. passport, and then we would fly back to Australia to be reunited as a family.

Even though we knew this separation was coming, it did not make the good-byes any easier. Our flights were scheduled within a few hours of each other, so we were able to wait together until boarding. All too soon, the time came. I hugged each of them one more time, then one more time, then, okay, *last time,* and they all kissed Lucy. Brian held Lucy as tight as she would let him, and kissed her little head. I yelled, "See you in two weeks!" My voice broke as I watched four pieces of my heart walk away, homeward bound.

"We got this, Lucy," I said, more for my sake than hers. The truth is, I was highly anxious about this part of the journey. Not only was I dreading flying internationally with my child whom I had only met ten days prior, but I also felt the pressure of tackling such crucially important items—citizenship, passport, social security card, Australian visa—all on my own.

Here are some thoughts I journaled in anticipation of this leg of the journey:

"Now, this is the part of the trip that makes my blood pressure rise. While in the States, I have two weeks to get Lucy a U.S. passport, apply for her Social Security card, and obtain a visa to get her into Australia. After hours of research by me and Lifeline and lots of phone calls to lots of government organizations, we should have everything in place to make this happen. If not, well, I just can't go there. On January 11th, Lord willing, my mom, Lucy, and I will fly back to Australia and our family will be together again and Lucy will finally be home."

I had no idea that our perfectly researched plan was about to be flipped on its head. A few days after we arrived in America, I wrote a blog entry that, despite my anxiety, I never in a million years anticipated writing.

December 30, 2013

I'm not sleeping much these days.

The combination of Lucy's jetlag plus my own has created nights of jilted sleep, at best. Girlfriend's favorite game these nights is "chicken." She wakes up in the middle of the night; I calm her down by rubbing her belly and humming to her while she lays in her crib. She starts her sleepy dance of patting her head and sucking her tongue, and her eyes dare me to walk away.

There is a pivotal moment when I can walk away without her crying again, but she gives me no real clue as to when this is. It's all a gamble. Her sweet face says, "Go back to bed; I'm good now." Then, the moment I step away, her scream says, "Sucker!!" The game begins again, and continues until I miraculously get the timing just right and can steal a few more hours of sleep.

When I said goodbye to the rest of my family Christmas night in the Guangzhou airport and walked down the jet way, just me and Lucy-Lu (at which point I wanted to yell, "Nooooo! Don't leave me!"), I anticipated the upcoming exhaustion, but really, I had no idea.

At first, I thought I was going to get off easy. Lucy fell asleep thirty minutes after takeoff, I laid her in the wall-mounted bassinet, and, shockingly, I didn't hear a peep from her for the next ten hours. Score! She woke up, drank a bottle, played a little bit, and boom, we were in Los Angeles. My row-mates were pleasantly surprised, especially since they took a look at us as we boarded the plane and desperately tried to find other seats. Good thing I'm so secure.

"The worst is over; piece of cake!" I thought. My Dad met me in L.A., and I thought it was all smooth sailing from there. We boarded the red-eye flight to Atlanta, and the sea got rocky. Just as people were settling in to sleep the flight away, Lucy started wailing. And wailing. She literally screamed for ninety

percent of the longest four hours of my life. Did I mention it was Christmas night? My apologies to everyone on board that fateful Delta flight for shattering your expectations of "Merry Christmas to all, and to all a good night." It was more like, "Hunker down for the worst Christmas night of your life."

At one point, a lady leaned over and actually told me Lucy was crying because I was holding her wrong. "Here, give her to me," she said, with a crazed, sleep-deprived glare. My child's incessant shrieking actually caused this poor woman to lose her mind. I gave an emphatic "No thanks," but what I wanted to say was, "Ma'am, this sweet thing was adopted a week and a half ago, has already traveled for twenty hours, and is constipated like you wouldn't believe. But I'm sure I'm just holding her wrong."

Somehow, we survived that flight and the next one to Memphis, and had a delightful reunion and first meeting with family. I forgave Lucy for her screaming, and she forgave me for putting her in a flying metal tube for thirty plus hours.

The very next day we loaded up and drove to the passport agency to accomplish the most crucial task of our time in America—getting Lucy a United States passport. In preparation for this day, I gathered documents, spoke to people at the National Passport Center, and talked multiple times to my social worker, all with the purpose of making sure that I had exactly what I needed to ensure that Lucy got a passport in time for us to fly back to Australia on January 11th.

I checked, re-checked, and obsessively-compulsively checked. Yet, I was still nervous walking through those doors. And for good reason. The agent had some questions about Lucy's visa and the fact that we live abroad, and said she would get back with us in a few days. We left with no passport—just more knots in my stomach.

A few days later, the agent called with the news that confirmed my worst fear: they would not issue Lucy a passport.

Despite the fact that we did everything by the books and provided all the documentation we were told was necessary, this particular agent had a problem with the fact that we were living abroad. Despite my pleas for her to understand and consider previous cases where this has not been an issue, for her to realize that the rest of my family was on the other side of the world and she was making it impossible for us to get to them, she would not budge.

I hung up the phone and sobbed.

Thankfully, one of the best places to be when you hit rock bottom is with people who love you. My parents, sister, and grandmother were there to hug me, encourage me, and cry with me. My grandmother loved me in the way that only grandmothers can. She held me tightly and said, "Do you want something to eat?"

I think of my friend Dianna who was stuck in Uganda for a month, apart from her family, while she was fighting for a visa to get her new son home, or my friend Michelle who endured living in Nicaragua for four months while she petitioned for her two new girls. My situation is nothing compared to theirs. If Lucy and I are stuck for a while, at least we're not stuck in China, and we're surrounded by people who love us.

But it doesn't make it any easier.

The agent is demanding Lucy's Certificate of Citizenship, which won't come in the mail for several months. Even though Lucy's visa was the type that grants citizenship upon entry into the U.S., this agent won't recognize it until she sees the certificate.

I'll be honest. As much as I love my parents and sister and all things America, I don't want to be away from Brian and the other kids for months on end. I don't want to miss their first day of school (the Australian school year begins at the end of January). I don't want to pay the crazy fees that are involved in changing an international plane ticket. I don't want Brian to miss any more time with his girl. I want him to be able to witness, as I am, the amazing progress Lucy is making.

Every time I read this blog entry, I feel the punch in my stomach once again. It reminds me of how, as children, my sister and I would run down our play set's slide, leap into the air, and grab onto an overhanging limb of a nearby tree. We did it over and over again. One day, it was not so magical. I ran down the slide, just like I'd done dozens of times before, jumped with arms outstretched, and missed the limb. Like a flying squirrel, I careened to the ground and hit belly-side down at full speed. I think that's the only time in my life when I literally had the wind knocked out of me. I rolled around on the ground groaning until my sister stopped laughing long enough to help me.

The denial of Lucy's passport felt a lot like my flying squirrel leap gone wrong. Just like I'd run down that slide problem-free many times before, hundreds of ex-pat families had gone before me and received passports for their newly adopted children without a hitch. I had every reason to believe this would be our experience as well. Yet, for some reason, this time the answer for us was no, and we were completely blindsided.

This day was one of the hardest, most disbelieving moments of my life. I had feared possible delays in getting Lucy a passport. Maybe the expedited process of getting a passport would take longer than two weeks, but for her actually to be denied a passport, even though she was a U.S. citizen? It was unthinkable. It was as if I were hearing the words through a heavy fog: "I'm sorry Mrs. Phillips, but we are unable to accept the application for your daughter's passport." It just didn't make sense.

"Are you telling me you're not going to issue my newly adopted daughter, who according to my understanding became a U.S. citizen upon entry into the United States, a passport?"

Shock quickly changed to disbelief, to anger, and then to despair.

I pleaded again. "Ma'am, I made sure we met all the requirements and filled out everything correctly. I said good-bye to my husband and three small children at the Guangzhou airport and told them I'd see them in two weeks. Hundreds of ex-pat families have gone before us, followed the exact same procedure, and were granted passports without any problem. What do you mean Lucy can't have a passport??"

"We will not issue the passport."

I was absolutely devastated and so very angry. How could this be?

The Lord brought this passage to mind: *"A man's heart devises his way: but the LORD directs his steps" (Proverbs 16:9).* But my plan was a good one, Lord! Straightforward, well researched, by the book, painless.

Yes, the journey I will always desire is a straight line, because that is the shortest distance between two points, right? But the twists, dips, and turns are what cause me to fall on my face before my Father, the ultimate Map Maker, a most-trusted Guide. After all, the journey is His story to tell.

Boy, was I ever going to fall on my face—over and over again. The journey had only just begun.

Chapter 10

Almost Famous

The denial of Lucy's passport sent shockwaves not only through our family, but through our adoption agency as well. No one was reeling more than our Lifeline social worker, Karla.

Let's just pause and talk about Karla for a moment, shall we?

Karla was on our team, cheering us on, from the very first inquiry we sent to the adoption agency asking if adoption as ex-pats were possible in Australia. She held our hands and walked with us through every step, every form, and all of my 5,234 idiotic questions. My emails to Karla usually went something like this: *"Karla, I am so high maintenance. I don't know why you put up with me. How the heck do I answer x question on form blah-blah-blah?"*

She always answered promptly and graciously, assuring me that no question was a dumb question, but let's face it—there are dumb questions, and I asked a lot of them. Our case required a lot of extra work on her part, as there were unique intricacies about adopting from Australia through the American system. Yet her feathers were never ruffled, and she often worked in the wee hours of the morning to make sure everything was done correctly and in a timely fashion. She has the calmest, most reassuring voice, something I would appreciate more and more as our journey continued. Put simply, she is the best.

Prior to the adoption trip, Karla and I had numerous conversations regarding my and Lucy's time in America. I can't count the number of times I would jokingly say, "Karla, I don't want to get stuck away from my family. How can I avoid getting stuck?" We would laugh, and she assured me that the process had been done smoothly hundreds of times before, and I was simply following in the footsteps of years of precedence. Lucy would obtain U.S. citizenship automatically upon entry into the States; therefore, she was entitled to a U.S. passport. All we had to do was submit the adoption decree, her birth certificate, and her Chinese passport, along with a few other forms, and we would be on our way. This process had been followed by literally hundreds of ex-pat families, and not just with our agency. Families of other agencies followed this protocol seamlessly as well.

So, while Karla was anxious to hear from me about our passport appointment, she never in a million years expected to hear my panicked voice on the other end of the phone telling her there would be no passport. She was shocked to say the least, and so burdened for me. Karla jumped into Emergency Mode and attacked the problem full force, immediately calling the passport agent who denied the application. This conversation did not go well.

The agent's stance, which she claimed was backed up by the legal department at Department of State, was that although Lucy lawfully entered the United States on the correct visa (which by definition grants automatic U.S. citizenship upon lawful entry), she also traveled in with a particular status which is intended for permanent residence. She claimed that because Lucy did not enter the States with the intention of permanent residence, she was not guaranteed automatic citizenship, and therefore could not be issued a passport. When Karla informed her that no other Lifeline ex-pat families ever had an issue obtaining automatic citizenship or a passport, her reply was, "Well, then all of those families were processed in error."

Really? For years and years, the State Department and Immigration got it wrong, but all of a sudden they decided to get it right with our case? It just did not add up.

One of the ironies in the whole situation was that even if residency were a factor, we had more evidence of residency than any other ex-pat family whom Lifeline had helped. Although we were living in Australia on a four year work visa, we still owned a home in Alabama, paid state and federal taxes, were employed by an American organization, were paid in U.S. dollars, and returned to the States every year. All evidence pointed to the fact that we still considered America our home. *(We would later find out that the term "permanent residence" was open to subjective interpretation, resulting in a variety of opinions from various government officials.)*

Karla appealed to the Department of Children's Issues within the Department of State, and the officer agreed with us. Of course Lucy should be granted a passport, she said. According to this officer, the stamp on Lucy's Chinese passport received by Immigration in Los Angeles was evidence of lawful entry, and the residence issue did not matter. We were hopeful and passed this information on to the passport agent, but she still would not budge. She said residence *was* an issue, and she would not issue the passport until she saw Lucy's Certificate of Citizenship, a document that wouldn't come for months. Her response meant that, unless someone intervened, Lucy and I would be separated from the rest of our family indefinitely.

Stuck away from my family! The thing I'd feared the most was coming true.

As each day passed, the plot thickened, and more people got involved with our case. Karla worked the phones with Department of State. Alabama Congressman Spencer Bachus' office began to apply political pressure. Tennessee Senators Alexander and Corker joined the scene. Family and friends called their Congressmen and pleaded our case. My parents' house was like a War Room, with all of us constantly working the computer and phones.

Oh, and by the way, this was all happening during a critical window of bonding between Lucy and me. While I should have been focusing all my attention on her, I was glued to my phone and email, fighting to get us home. It was not ideal. During one conversation with the passport agent, she said, "Well, it's good that you're getting some extra bonding time with your daughter." I was like, "Um, it's difficult to focus on bonding when you're so completely stressed about not being able to get home to the rest of your family." That was a conversation stopper.

Meanwhile, my blog and Facebook blew up, and people came out of the woodwork to help. Our story just seemed implausible: "American missionary family separated by half the globe as newly adopted child is denied an American passport." *What?* I mean, it's horrible but not surprising when adoption-related immigration hiccups occur in other countries, but in the good ol' U S of A, to a child who should be an American citizen? Unthinkable. Much to my disbelief, thousands of people began to follow our story. Perhaps for me, it was a case of "Be careful what you wish for"? Hmmm.

January 2nd, 2014

My whole life, I've wanted to be famous.

I'm a good singer, but as a child I thought I was a fantastic singer. I can remember sitting in the bathtub, practicing my part of future duets that I would one day sing on the big stage with my favorite singers, which at that time were the great Sandi Patty and Larnelle Harris. I was what you would call a sheltered child.

I've also dreamed of being in the movies, even though my acting experience is limited to playing an incognito female Civil War soldier for a three-minute production at Girl's State during my junior year of high school. I mean, when I pulled off my beret and dramatically shook out my hair, revealing I was a girl, and saluted the ol' red, white, and blue, it was shock and awe. I don't think there was a dry eye in the house. I tear up just thinking about it.

I may or may not have recurring dreams about singing on American Idol, *and on an anniversary trip to NYC, I made it my goal to be on TV as many times as possible. You may remember me from the* Today *show.*

Despite my silly ambitions, I can honestly say that I never imagined I would become semi-famous for being "The Girl and Her Newly Adopted Child Who are Stuck in America and Can't Get Home to Their Family." Not the title I was looking for. "Best Actress," maybe, "Best New Artist," absolutely—but not this one.

The past three days, there has been a flurry of activity on the part of our family, Lifeline Children's Services, and so many others to get a passport for Lucy. Congressmen and Senators have been brought into the mix, officers in the Department of State have been lobbying for us, and anyone who has any kind of political contacts has passed these on to us or contacted the statesmen themselves. I feel like we're days away from holding a press conference. (Not really. I don't think. Nah . . .)

I, and many of you, prayed that we would get word TODAY that Lucy's passport had been approved.

It didn't happen.

I can't say I am not disappointed, but I'm also not in despair. Here are two major things I have learned from this experience so far:

1) It's an awful thing to be a victim of injustice, and people all over the world experience injustice every single day.

It physically hurts to think Lucy and I potentially could be apart from my other three kids and Brian for a long period of time, but there are immigrants worldwide who are apart from their families unjustly for months, years, or even decades without the resources that we have. This is not a new problem; I just never thought it would happen to me.

I can't help but be reminded of the One who faced the most injustice of all. Jesus was separated from His Father, arrested in innocence, and put to death even though He was without guilt. He knows what it is like to be punished despite doing the right thing. Hebrews says I don't have a High Priest who is unable to sympathize with my weaknesses, and this week, I get that. He understands, and He is interceding and fighting on my behalf.

2) It's a precious thing to be loved.

Brian and I have been so overwhelmed by the support, love, and prayers we've received over this whole adoption journey, and especially over these last few days. God has loved us through your emails, messages, phone calls, and efforts to contact anyone and everyone that you think could possibly help us. We are so humbled that you would love our family, and especially our sweet little Lucy, so much.

We continue to wait. My hope and prayer is that tomorrow is the day. Wouldn't that be awesome? In the meantime, I'll try not to let the fame get to my head, I'll fight to trust my Savior who holds all things together, and I'll soak up my Little Treasure.

So, I got my wish. I was kind of famous. Yet, despite my love for drama, this was one scene I didn't want to star in. I was ready for the Director to call, "Cut! That's a wrap!" and we could all go home. It didn't play out that way. Instead, I remained the star of my own *Stuck* documentary, thereby identifying with every other person who had ever been stuck. I could see no way out.

Super Karla reminded me, "All miracles begin with a crisis." Yes, that's true. Only people who are stuck can experience the thrill of being rescued. So, I continued to pray that The Miracle would cease to elude me, ushering in the Day of Rescue. "The Girl Who Was Dramatically Rescued From Immigration Nightmare"? Now *that's* a good reason to be famous.

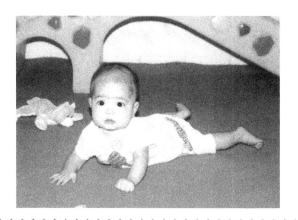

The first picture we received of beautiful Lucy

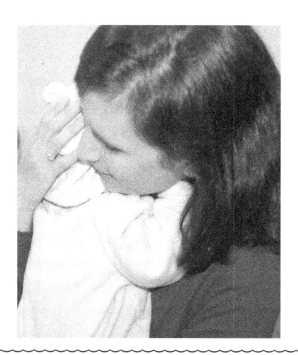

Gotcha Lucy. Sweet first snuggles with my girl.

Presenting Phillips, party of six!

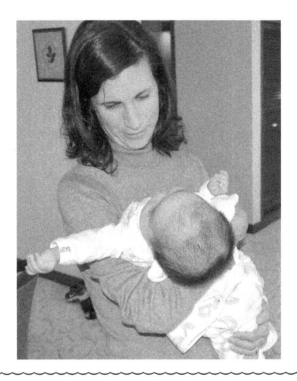

Lucy's position of choice while we were in China—leaning back as far as she could go.

After only having her for a few days, we coaxed this giggle out of her.

Brian saying good-bye to his baby girl in Guangzhou before our family parted ways.

Face Timing with Daddy—part of our daily routine.

Learning to crawl

Our faces say it all. Discouraged, sad, ready to be together again.

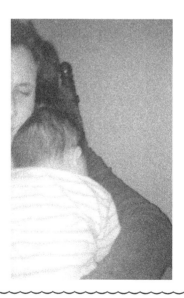

A miraculous night. For the first time, Lucy leaned in with trust, and slept.

Chapter 11

Broken

T hey call it the Fog of War. When you're in the middle of a battle, literally or figuratively, information flies as fast as bullets, yet much gets lost in translation due to the chaotic nature of the circumstances. It's hard to know what is true, what is merely perception, and what's simply a fragment of the truth that has been tainted by fear and emotion.

This first week of Operation Get Lucy a Passport was very much a War Fog. The passport agent continued to insist the law supported her decision to deny the passport, but other information and opinions kept flying in from all directions, all of them giving us more confidence to believe that we were in the right—that Lucy was legally qualified for a passport.

Lawyers told us so, and wanted to start a campaign with the title, "American citizen denied U.S. passport." An officer with Department of State said that while the residency issue can be grey for ex-pats, Lucy's visa still qualified her for automatic citizenship, and thus a passport. The adoption agency was in contact with this officer daily, and she seemed confident that this would all be resolved quickly. Years of precedence told us we were in the right. In fact, another missionary family had entered the States just two weeks before us, got their child's passport within two days, and returned to the country where they were stationed, no questions asked. Yet we were being detained. Makes perfect sense, right?

Karla and I made daily phone calls to our friend the Passport Agent, with whom we would plead on all kinds of levels. One of my strongest arguments was that in preparation for travel, I made several calls to the National Passport Agency to ensure I understood the correct procedure to get Lucy's passport. In these calls, I made it clear that we were living abroad, and that I would not have Lucy's Certificate of Citizenship when I applied for the passport. I was assured it would not be a problem, and that Lucy would definitely be granted a passport. The information they gave me was not unique to me. Another missionary family who was investigating how to get a passport for their newly adopted child received this reply to their inquiry to the National Passport Center:

Required Documentation for a U.S. Passport:

To obtain a passport a customer must submit the following original documents; photocopies are not acceptable. A formal or informal English translation of foreign documents is also required.

1. Child's foreign Birth Certificate OR if adopted/re-adopted in the United States, the state-issued birth certificate with the seal from the issuing authority OR

2. Certified copy of Childs' foreign Adoption Decree

3. Parents' evidence of U.S. Citizenship

4. Child's evidence of lawful admission

> * Foreign passport with USCIS stamp I-551 OR
> * Permanent Resident Card

5. Parents' certified Marriage Certificate, if applicable

6. Parents' certified Divorce, Separation or legal Custody Decree, if applicable

NOTE: The customer may submit a Certificate of Citizenship in place of the above documents.

We provided the appropriate documents. According to this response, the Certificate of Citizenship was not necessary. More evidence in our favor.

When I relayed all of this information to the agent who had denied us, her reply was firm: "The National Passport Center is simply an information center. They don't make decisions on individual cases." My indignant response: "I'm sorry; don't you call an information center to get information? And don't you trust that the information they're giving you is correct?" Through tears, I reminded her again that her decision was causing my newly adopted, special needs child and me to be separated from my husband and other three small children. Would she please show some mercy? We're talking about a thirteen-pound, fifteen-month-old baby, not a security threat, for crying out loud! The result? No compassion, no wavering, no mercy. No passport.

"Just let your daughter travel to Australia on her Chinese passport," the agent said, "and get her U.S. passport whenever you move back to America." A simple thing to suggest; a very unwise decision to carry out. The U.S. Consulate in Guangzhou strongly urged us never to use our child's Chinese passport again, because China does not recognize dual citizenship. Besides, Lucy travelling on a Chinese passport would make things complicated on the Australian immigration end, so it was a risk we couldn't take.

We had to get that American passport.

Despite the brick wall we kept hitting with the passport agent, the weekend was quickly approaching, and Super Karla and I were more than hopeful that we would have a resolution by Friday. Everyone wants to clear his desk before the weekend, right? Congressmen were putting pressure on the right people, the State Department seemed to be on our side, and we had a lot of people praying. If I just had enough faith, it would all work out.

Except it didn't—not that week.

Without even realizing it, I became engaged in a battle much bigger than the fight for a passport. I was fighting to base my faith on the surety of Christ and not on my circumstances, and I was failing miserably. I found my emotions heavily dependent upon the news I did or did not receive each day. Those of you who have ever fallen into that trap know that it's exhausting. I do not recommend it.

I would get an encouraging email from a politician and become elated, but then run into a dead end five minutes later and fall apart. I had faced Tough Life Stuff before, but I thought I was much stronger than this. I wasn't. I was Peter, looking at the tempestuous waves and sinking fast. I was a broken mess, and in my own understanding, I was running out of time.

January 3rd, 2014

Faith can be a fragile thing.

Yesterday, although we didn't have any great news about Lucy's passport, I still felt hopeful. We had some strong leads going into today, and I really thought today was The Day. This ridiculous nightmare would end, and Lucy and I would be free to enjoy the rest of our time with family, looking forward to reuniting with Brian and the kids in just one week.

As the day went on, each lead weakened and the prospects looked bleak. Even though all of those leads were sympathetic to our situation, no one seemed able to intervene and make this right. The nail in the coffin came when a twenty-minute conversation with a supervisor who I thought would finally be able to do something about this problem ended with my being directed back to the passport agent who denied us in the first place. And she's not relenting.

I would love to say that my faith is not based on circumstances, that I can steadily, unwaveringly trust the Lord no matter what. The truth is revealed in the fact that yesterday I could see the comedy in our situation, mainly because I really thought it would be resolved within the next twenty-four hours.

Today, I wept.

My text to my dear friend Bek went something like this: "Has your faith ever felt so weak that you needed others to believe for you? That is today."

That's the truth. I have never felt so trapped, helpless, or suffocated by a reality that I can't fix. I know what's true—that God loves me extravagantly, that His purposes will prevail, that He wouldn't have led us on this adoption journey to not carry it to completion, but the knots in my stomach are still there. The fear still chokes me.

As I'm tempted to submerge myself in despair, I remember Peter's desperate words when Jesus asked if he, too, would leave Him. "To whom shall we go? You have the words of eternal life" (John 6:68). Words of life such as these:

"Some trust in chariots, and some in horses: but we will remember the name of the LORD our God" (Psalms 20:7).

"For the mountains shall depart, and the hills be removed; but my kindness will not depart from you, neither will the covenant of my peace be removed, says the LORD that has mercy on you" (Isaiah 54:10).

"But my God shall supply all your need according to his riches in glory by Christ Jesus" (Philippians 4:19).

So, when I Skype with my family, and the kids show me the calendar they made, marking off the days until Lucy and I come home next week, because they still think that's the plan; when I'm ending my chat time with them and Sarah Kate says, "Don't press 'end' Mommy—please don't press 'end,'" and it is more than I can take, I'll go back to the Words of Life, or I'll ask someone else to take me there.

I'll stand on the faith of others who believe for me when I don't have the strength to believe for myself. I will believe that

God is good, and that one day soon, instead of blowing kisses to a screen, I'll have my husband and all my kids physically in my arms, and all will feel right again.

This situation was humbling, to say the least, for someone who has been a Christian for most of her life. I didn't want to be broken. I wanted to be a stalwart—unmoving, undeterred, come what may. But really, the only One who fits that description is Jesus. He is the only One who could fully experience very real human emotions of pain, sadness, and righteous anger, yet never waver—not for a second—in His assurance that His Father truly knew best.

Yes, He asked for His circumstances to change, but what He wanted more than that was for His Father's will to be done. He could sleep like a baby in the fiercest of storms because He trusted the One who simultaneously formed the waves and held the boat together.

Only Jesus could trust perfectly. I could not, but, like Peter, I was not abandoned in my unbelief. Instead, Jesus met me in the waves and pulled me to safety, over and over again. He did not tire of my humanity. Instead, He acted consistently with His character: He was a kind and patient Friend.

Chapter 12

When Life Turns Upside-Down

My daily "routine," if you can call it that, went something like this: Get awakened waaaayyyy too early by an "I'm still on China time" Lucy, feed her a bottle, play on the floor, and call Brian to update him on the progress, or lack thereof, with The Situation. Wait for business hours to begin, and start the mass phone call and email campaign anew. Attempt to bond with Lucy, help her overcome sensory issues, resolve her chronic constipation, and teach her to eat, all while fighting bureaucracies. I had to be the only one to do these things, because it was vital she bond to me and not my parents. I believe Karyn Purvis left out a crucial chapter in her book, *The Connected Child*: "Bonding with Your Child While On Hold With Government Agencies All Day Long." That would have been helpful.

I have to confess: I did find ways to relieve the stress. My coping mechanism is comedy, and my sister Julianne is my favorite person to laugh with, so it came in mighty handy that I was facing this crisis in her hometown.

Let me give some context about my sister, my fellow comedian. Once she watched me accidentally tip over a brand new Costco-sized bucket of Skittles, causing brightly colored beads of candy goodness to rain over my head and bounce all over the kitchen, and whispered behind me, "*Taste the rainbow*." She and I sing into mirrors together, harmonizing horribly and thanking the audience for coming ("Thank you, thank you, we're here all night.") We also love to parade around in awful puffy paint sweatshirts circa 1990 that we dig up at my parents' house. We think we are *hilarious.*

So, in order to cope with a horrible situation, she and I created this comedy bit where we imagined that this crazy immigration nightmare was changed into a made-for-TV movie. We had it all planned out: The backdrop would show congressmen's aides working the phones, Lifeline's staff madly rushing about, everyone in a panicked, fevered pitch, and then the words would pop onto the screen: "Meanwhile, back in Lakeland . . ." (Lakeland is a Memphis suburb where my parents lived, and where Lucy and I were camping out.)

Clips would flow onto the screen of my sister and me acting out the mindless activities we had been doing to escape the stress, such as eating all my favorite take-out foods that my sister delivered to me every other day via her SUV, or as I called it, her Food Truck; watching Jimmy Fallon videos one after the other, especially "Thank You Notes"; me texting her at 10:30 p.m. to let her know that the stars had aligned and Jimmy Fallon *and* Justin Timberlake were both on *Saturday Night Live*, and then me trying not to wake my parents with raucous laughter.

We had the cast picked as well. Of course, I would play myself, Jennifer Aniston would play my sister (they do share the same birthday, after all), and the great Jimmy Fallon himself would play Brian, obviously. I still think it could work.

As great as these moments of laughter were, they were simply moments, and did not ease the unavoidable pain of the daily Skype sessions with my other three kids. Each afternoon, as business hours were closing and I faced the end of yet another day without answers, the kids would just be waking up in Australia, and were ready to talk to Mom. Each day, I had to answer their questions with, "No news today. I'm so sorry." Then I would encourage them to keep praying.

This crisis was the first major problem that our family had personally faced, and it was tricky to know how to navigate it theologically. We wanted to trust God for big things, and we wanted the kids to step out in faith and pray expectantly, but what if He didn't answer the way we wanted Him to? What if Lucy and I *were not* on that January eleventh flight? The kids started to wonder the same thing.

January 5ᵗʰ, 2014

"Mommy, at church today, I asked my teacher to pray for a passport for Lucy," Sarah Kate says. I smile. "Thanks sweetheart. I think there are hundreds of people praying for Lucy's passport. I just know God is going to answer."

"But what if He doesn't?"

There you have it. That question. The one that addresses the messy mix of the power of our prayers and God's sovereignty. How do we pray confidently and specifically, standing on God's promises, without our faith being destroyed if God doesn't answer the way in which we're hoping?

*Our friends Shadrach, Meshach, and Abednego faced this very dilemma. When this trio was about to be thrown into the fiery furnace, they emphatically claimed God's physical protection: "Our God whom we serve is able to deliver us from the burning fiery furnace, and he will deliver us out of your hand, O king." Super confident, huh? Fully trusting in the fact that God was able to rescue them, and that He would do it. Dangerous territory, some may say. You're just setting yourself up for disappointment. But they go on—and this is the key— "**But if not,** be it known unto you, O king, that we will not serve your gods" (Daniel 3:17-18).*

Here's the deal: I want to be on that airplane with Lucy in arms on Saturday. I am fervently praying and trusting God to do just that. Many of you have prayed for me when I didn't have the strength or words to pray myself. I am pleading with you to continue to stand in the gap and pray all the more fervently that this situation is resolved within the next few days, and that this time next week, I'll be reunited with the rest of my family. Period.

But even if He does not.

Oh, this is hard, but He's still good. He's still in control. I won't worship another because my following Christ isn't dependent upon His doing what I want Him to do. If time runs out and my stay here is extended indefinitely, would I experience the very real human emotions of disappointment, grief, even devastation? Yes. I can't even let my mind go there. But it doesn't mean He's not real or that He does not care. It actually means He sees a picture and a purpose that I can't see.

But even if He does not, He'll meet me there as well.

God did continue to meet me as the hourglass wound down. It actually seemed as if we were going to get our miracle. One of the congressional aides who had been helping us made contact with a USCIS official in Atlanta who confirmed that we were in the right. Lucy should be granted a passport. However, since the passport agent refused to approve the application without seeing Lucy's Certificate of Citizenship, the USCIS official advised the government aide to request an expedited certificate from the processing center in Buffalo, New York.

This was it! The answer we'd been waiting for! The processing center would learn that a congressman was requesting an expedited process, the certificate would be printed and overnighted to us, and we'd hit the highway and be at the passport office the same day. The application would be approved, the prized passport would be printed, and Lucy and I would make our flight. We hit our knees, the congressional aide hit the phones . . . and they just rang and rang.

Would you believe that a Polar Vortex, aka massive winter storm, had basically shut down the city of Buffalo? Yes it did. The countdown calendar was being eaten up with public holidays and snow days, and there wasn't much time left. Would God come through for us? Or was His definition of "coming through" different than mine?

January 8th, 2014

"For as the heavens are higher than the earth, so are my ways higher than your ways, and my thoughts than your thoughts" (Isaiah 55:9).

In my limited understanding, today would have been a good day to get a passport. I mean, it was all-systems go: an immigration official confirming that the passport agent was in error, a Congressman giving the green light and requesting an emergency Certificate of Citizenship, a crazy number of people praying. All the processing center has to do is push print and get that bad boy on the next FedEx plane, right? It's the perfect ending to the story that refuses to end!

Except no one is answering the phone or emails at the processing center, because it's in Buffalo, NY. In case you haven't been paying attention to the weather, they were hit big time by a Polar Vortex. Instead of processing COC's, those workers are home cuddling in their Snuggies and sipping hot chocolate. Not that I blame them, but seriously, I needed them on the job today.

Another day down, two to go. You would think I would be panicking right now, but honestly, today—in this moment—I'm at peace. Everywhere I turn, left and right, are reminders that I am not in control. I cannot fix this. I don't control the heart of a stubborn passport agent. I don't control the weather. I don't control my grandmother getting sick and going into the hospital this week, taking my mom away from us for several days, and shaking an already shaky plan of her flying home with me on Saturday.

As a government official told me today, off the record, "Jennifer, God is in control. If He wants you on that plane on Saturday, you will be."

So, today, I'm experiencing the "peace of God which passes all understanding" (Philippians 4:7), because honestly, it doesn't make sense that I would have peace. Peace comes from following the commands of the previous verses: "Be careful for nothing; but in everything by prayer and supplication with thanksgiving let your requests be made known to God" (Philippians 4:6).

My requests have been made known to my Father—by me and by hundreds of you. Now it's time to give thanks:

- I'm thankful for my husband Brian who has faithfully, tirelessly cared for our oldest three children for the last fifteen days. He has taken up the role of Fun Captain in my absence, and has taken them to the movies, taken them swimming, and even held singing competitions to the Frozen soundtrack. (This was videotaped, and he definitely has a solo. I must find a way to get it on YouTube.) Although he has been helpless to help logistically with this fight to get us home, he has ministered to me by loving our children abundantly, and by organizing our craft cupboard. He rocks.
- I'm thankful for Joshua, Andrew, and Sarah Kate, three of my greatest joys. They have been superstars these last two weeks, and have jumped on board with Dad's new chore chart like champs. What can I say? Brian likes to organize. Perhaps I should go away more often? Sorry—not funny—too soon.
- I'm thankful for my Mom, who I found in the dark, in the middle of the night, praying for me. I'm thankful for my Dad for literally being willing to do whatever it takes to get Lucy a passport.
- I'm thankful for my sister, my best hood rat, who distracts me with Jimmy Fallon videos so I can do something other than stare at the phone and will it to ring.

- *I'm thankful for amazing friends who planned a special lunch for Lucy and me today, who oohed and ahhed over her, and who blessed me with the security of their lifelong friendship.*
- *I'm thankful for Chick-fil-A sweet tea, and my even sweeter friend Mandy who bought me a gallon of it.*
- *I'm thankful for the prayers of hundreds of people who have followed this story.*
- *I'm thankful for Karla, the world's greatest adoption social worker, who has been on the front lines on my behalf around the clock. I'm thankful for her calm, sweet voice on the other end of the phone.*
- *I'm thankful for my little Lucy. Her life is a miracle, and the privilege of loving light and life into her eyes is too great to describe.*
- *Most of all, I'm thankful for Jesus, who is my hope.*

Chapter 13

Not Where We Planned to Be

January 10ᵗʰ, 2014

Okay, deep breaths. This one is hard to write.

I so wanted to use this space today to tell all about the miracle that God did to enable Lucy and me to go home tomorrow. All day I played out the possible scenarios. Would it be the last minute phone call from the Congressman, saying the Certificate of Citizenship had been emailed to Arkansas? Maybe the passport agent saying she had reversed her decision? Or perhaps it would be my Dad's final plea, after driving for hours to the agency, just in case.

But it was none of these. Three o'clock came and went. The agency closed. I cancelled the flights.

I know the past few days I've talked a lot about peace, and I do still have peace. But let me tell you what peace is not. Peace is not the absence of pain. Today, I know that full well. My heart is broken, heavy with the burden of telling my children, "No, I'm not coming home tomorrow, and I'm sorry sweetheart, I don't know when."

None of this makes sense. I don't know why God didn't give us that miracle that we were all praying for today. I do know this: Today I prayed, "Lord, if You will get the most glory by showing up big and getting me on that plane, then do it, but if You'll receive more glory by my remaining and continuing to walk, stumbling, on this journey, then that's okay too."

God is good, but today, submission hurts.

It was not the ending I was hoping for.

Maybe I'd seen too many movies. Maybe false realities of last-minute interventions had become my framework for how life should actually play out. Or perhaps it was just my penchant for drama? Whatever the reason, I truly thought that at the midnight hour, our miracle would arrive, and the day would be saved.

My mom, Lucy, and I had tickets to fly out on Saturday, January eleventh. On Thursday the ninth, the passport agent told me that she had asked the legal department at Department of State to review our case, and that she should hear from them by the next morning (Friday). In the meantime, congressional aides continued to try to make contact with the Buffalo USCIS service center to request the expedited Certificate of Citizenship.

Friday was our last hope to make those flights. Even though my Dad, a seminary professor, had classes to teach, he decided to leave Friday morning to make the long drive to the passport agency, *just in case* the legal department overturned the passport agent's decision, or *just in case* we got through to Buffalo and they were able to email a scanned copy of the COC to the passport office. My Dad is amazing. I mean, who does that? Driving for hours on end, just in case? This is the same man who drove eight hours to my junior high camp to bring me a cake, because he was afraid I wouldn't feel special enough on my birthday. He's the best.

As Dad flew down the highway, I waited by the phone for news, any news. The hours clicked by all too slowly and all too quickly at the same time. It was an excruciating wait. In the end, the legal department did not render a decision and the Buffalo center couldn't be reached. My Dad arrived at the passport office thirty minutes before closing time, and was callously told to go home.

Time was up.

This wasn't the way it was supposed to go! This beautiful adoption story was supposed to have a happy ending. My kids' countdown calendar said I was flying home on Saturday and I had every right to be on that plane! I had written each of the kids a note for each day I would be away from them, and there were only fourteen notes. Their last note read, "See you tomorrow!" This new reality was making my note a lie, and I'm not in favor of lying to my kids.

What about all the people who had been following our story and praying for us? Friends of mine who were shaky in their faiths were praying for a miracle. Wouldn't a miracle be just the thing to strengthen their beliefs in a God who can and will do big things? What about my friends who didn't believe in Jesus? Would this "no" not confirm their opinion that God either didn't exist or was simply cruel? Would my faith look like a sham?

On the flip side, friends who were, in my opinion, pillars of the faith were praying as well and were confident that we would get the answer we were hoping for. Why didn't God answer them? How could our family's separation, our inability to begin our New Beginning with Lucy, further God's kingdom? How could it be best for Lucy to experience her first crucial months with a single mom instead of a full family?

How could this be happening? I needed a shift in perspective.

One of my favorite Bible stories is about Jonah, but not the part about the whale. It's afterwards, when Jonah does what he's told to do and tells Nineveh to repent, and surprisingly, they actually do. What Jonah does next in response to their about-face seems incredibly self-centered, but I can relate. He climbs to the top of a hill, and tells God he's so angry that God forgave Nineveh that he just wants to die. God asks Jonah, "Do you have a right to be angry?" I feel like Jonah is channeling me when he says, "Yes, in fact, I do have a right to be angry." Then God sends scorching sun and winds and Jonah is angry, but when God provides a vine to protect Jonah, he's happy again. Because He can, God shrivels up the vine and Jonah's angry again and wants to die. God gently questions Jonah, "Do you have a right to be angry about the vine?"

Jonah again responds honestly and feistily, "Yes! Yes I have a right to be angry about the vine!" He was like, "Yes, God, you made it better, but then you made it worse again. I do have a case here. I want to be angry so I will be angry!"

God puts things into perspective: "Listen Jonah, you're super concerned about this plant that you didn't make grow, yet you don't think I should have pity on a city of a hundred thousand people who are going to destroy themselves in this life and the next if I don't intervene?" According to God, the Ninevites did not know their right hand from their left, which was a much bigger concern than Jonah's sense of justice or desire for comfort.

I was Jonah. I didn't like God's decision and I was angry and hurt. I felt that I deserved to feel this way. After all, justice was not served. What Lucy deserved was a passport, a ticket home, and a whole family to bond with. She deserved proper health care and therapies that would be covered under our insurance in Australia, but were not covered in America. She deserved to sleep in the nursery I so lovingly prepared for her months before. What I deserved was to be reunited with my husband and children on my previously determined timeline. I *did* have a right to be angry. I did.

Yet, as a friend of mine whose wife and daughter were critically injured in a car accident said, "Is life simply about the avoidance of pain, or is it about something else?" God sees the bigger picture. Although we want life to be about pain avoidance, if we want to experience Christ more richly, it must be about something else.

This trial was the pain that was chosen for us, and Lucy and I were not going to get on that plane because God did not want us on that plane, not that day. A bigger purpose was being served that we couldn't see, and even though it was painfully hard, submission was key. God chose to give us a stage on which to display not the strength of our faith, but the splendor of His glory. It was not the path we would have chosen, and we would have given anything to make things different, but we could submit because we trusted Him and His unchanging character.

By the way, sometimes, by not meeting our felt need, God actually meets our spiritual need. I thought I needed a passport; God knew I needed to be broken. He knew I needed to be strengthened in my dependence on Him, in my ability to trust beyond what I could see. Even though the circumstances were painful, our God was and is in control, and that reassurance kept me walking on that rocky path instead of deserting it altogether.

Chapter 14

Still Worth It?

With the deadline of booked flights past, reality set in that Lucy and I could be in America for much longer than the planned two weeks. Brian and the kids couldn't easily get to us, as that would mean thousands of dollars and their missing the start of school, and Lucy and I couldn't get to them. God was asking me to continue to care for this child on my own, a child whose affections I had yet to win.

It's a peculiar thing to love a child who does not love you back. When a child grows in your womb, she is part of you. You speak to her, you feed her, you nurture her. You are familiar to her. The first time she's placed on your chest, she naturally snuggles up. Of course, she doesn't have the muscle tone or coordination yet to try to move away from you, but even if she did, she wouldn't want to. A newborn's body naturally curves onto yours as she leans in, not away, for reassurance. She may cry, but she nestles against you for comfort. Being apart from you is scary and unknown; being held by you is home.

Lucy and I did not get the privilege of this natural form of bonding. She and I missed out on crucial months of stroking, rocking, singing, and cuddling. Left alone for most hours of the day on a wooden slat that cruelly pretended to be a bed, she soothed herself with tapping or tongue sucking. She had no one else.

Then I entered the scene fifteen months later and wanted to hold her. I wanted to kiss her and stroke her and cuddle her and give her all the things she'd missed out on for so very long.

I was not welcome.

I was a stranger, and because she was sensory-deprived, touch was almost painful. When I held her on my hip, she leaned her body back, hands in the air. Her newborn body never got the opportunity to nestle against the chest of someone who loved her, so she never learned how to lean in for comfort. Instead, she stiffened at my touch, her expression stoic. When she awoke from her nap, she didn't cry for me—not even when she had a soiled diaper. Why should she? When no one rushes to your side when you cry, you eventually stop crying. Lucy didn't know she needed me because her needs had never been met well. The concept of a mother was foreign to her.

I was so torn. My three biological children who *were* bonded to me, and had been since day one, were on one side of the world. My adopted daughter, who still didn't quite know what to think of me, was with me on the other. I felt so guilty for "abandoning" my older three who needed their Mom, yet I had been called to love one who had already experienced abandonment and was only beginning to heal.

Loving the three was easy; loving the one was hard.

Getting emails like this one from Joshua did not make things any easier:

Hi Mom.
We all miss you a lot, but I've found that it's been especially hard for me to go without you today. I miss your hugs, our "little talks," you scratching my back, your poppy-seed chicken, and everything else about you. I can't wait to talk to you tomorrow.
Your loving son,
Joshua

Talk about ripping your heart out. I read it over and over and cried each time. It was hard enough to hear my six-year-old little girl cry because I wasn't coming home. It was even harder to know that my ten-year-old tough guy was missing his Mom scratching his back at night.

When we made the decision to adopt, we knew it was going to be hard. We knew it would be messy and inconvenient. We invested hours of our time into education that told us that adoption would be one of the most difficult and most rewarding things we would ever undertake. We signed forms and agreements saying yes, we know this will not be easy. But did we really? As I stared down the barrel of indefinite separation from four of the loves of my life, I realized how shallow our understanding of "hard" had been.

January 12th, 2014

It's funny how so often we make bold statements before we have any idea what they mean.

On our wedding day, when I promised to love Brian 'til death do we part, I had a very limited understanding of what that meant. Up until that point, it meant mushy feelings and wrestling through tough issues like, "Should we register for Corning Ware or French Countryside?" and "Can he possibly ever learn to make birthdays and holidays as big of a deal as I want him to?" (He's come a long way, but we're still working on it. Gone are the days of him re-gifting to me gifts that I had previously given to him. No lie.)

I had no idea that loving this man, walking through life with him, would mean facing sick children, sleepless nights, us both being down for the count with stomach viruses that had us begging Jesus to take us now. I didn't know it would mean walking hand-in-hand through the long, dark valley of leaving everyone and everything we loved behind and moving to the other side of the world.

These same things that tested our love actually deepened our love, and defined the very commitment we so whimsically promised all those years ago.

When all we knew of Lucy was four pictures, a video, and a limited medical file, I mentioned countless times that she was worth it. Worth the paperwork, worth the adoption fees, worth whatever it would take to mean she was ours. Brian and I knew it would be hard, that it would change our family forever, but we emphatically claimed that she was worth it all.

Now, that statement is being tested.

Is she worth being separated from the rest of my family indefinitely? Is she worth the legal battles, the hours on the phone and computer, the enormous stress? I've recently been asked that if this battle over Lucy's citizenship and a passport continues on, would I consider leaving her here with family and returning for a time to Australia to be with Brian and the other kids? (Now, let me preface my answer with this: I have very dear friends who have had to do just this, because they literally had no choice, and it almost killed them. Their situations were horrible and I pass no judgment on the fact that they left; it was the only thing they could do. My situation is a little bit different.)

As I considered my own response to this question, I could understand why some people might think this is what I should do. I mean, I've only had Lucy for four weeks, and she's just getting used to me. Babies are resilient, and oh, the hero's welcome I would get at home. I can imagine my older kids' response: Sarah Kate would squeeze my neck as hard as she could. Andrew would give me lots of sloppy kisses. Joshua would sweetly say, "I've missed you, Mom." It would be such a relief to hold them again.

On the other hand, here, I have to fight every day for another tiny little piece of Lucy's heart. She doesn't give kisses and she doesn't know how to hug, keeping her hands defensively in the air most of the time that I hold her. In fact, it was a huge victory the other day when she actually rested her hand on my shoulder. Sometimes she would still rather lie in her crib than cry for me to come get her when she wakes up.

So, it makes sense for me to go home, right? Except, she's my child. Mine. God has given me a love for her that is just as intense as the love I have for my other three. This baby came to us traumatized and neglected. She has experienced abandonment once, and I cannot do it to her again. I can't undo the security she's just beginning to feel. I just can't.

In the book of Matthew, Jesus talks about the shepherd who leaves the ninety-nine to go after the one lost sheep. This choice would seem foolish to most, but Jesus is no ordinary shepherd. He knew the one was worth it. I was worth it. You are worth it.

So, is Lucy worth it? Even though she doesn't lavish me with affection, doesn't yet fully accept me? Even though she still pushes me away? Even though it means separation from the other loves of my life?

I look into those deep brown eyes, full of mystery, sorrow, and yet now, hope and light, and I say, absolutely. Our commitment to her is being tested to the fullest extent, but our answer is still yes. We would do it all over again.

I can honestly say this was true. When we said yes to Lucy, we agreed to lay our lives down for her—life as we knew it. There was no form to sign that said, "We'll sacrifice this part of our lives for her, but not that," or "We'll be inconvenienced up to a certain point, and then no more." No, we pursued her and said, "She will be ours, no matter what." Even though we never could have anticipated this version of "no matter what," it wasn't up to us to determine what version of hard we would get with Lucy.

In a world that so easily throws up its hands and says, "Too hard," and walks away, God was asking us to mirror His commitment to us by looking at sweet Lucy and saying, "Dear one, you are not too much for us. No cost is too high; no burden too much to bear. We will fight for you, because you are worth it."

Who knows? Maybe a day will come when Lucy walks through the pain of questions of identity. It's almost inevitable. Maybe one day she'll feel sad because she looks different than us, or maybe a peer will cruelly joke about her "real parents." Maybe it is for these moments that God created an opportunity for us to fight for her, for me to choose to stay with her rather than return to her adoptive siblings. Maybe God knew that there were weak times to come when she would need to know for sure that she is worth it.

I pray that she'll be able to look back and see that at a time when she offered me nothing, I sacrificed presence with those closest to me in order to love her and bring her home. I pray that the memory of that sacrifice would draw her eyes towards a Savior who also forfeited presence with the One closest to Him so that He could one day bring her home, for good.

Chapter 15

Hello, Desperation

I t's interesting how our minds hold the files of some memories so clearly, while others are blurred or discarded altogether. How do our brains choose? I heard one theory that you only remember the things from your childhood that are consistent with what you believe to be true about yourself. So, if you believe that you're a winner, you'll remember all those home runs, scored goals or prize-winning SAT scores in high definition, while your failures are not so clear. Alternately, if you have a low self-image, your failures are heightened in your memory, blocking out any successes you may have obtained.

In keeping with that theory, I'm not sure what it says about me that I have a crystal clear image of one particular day in the fourth grade. My mom was a teacher at my school, so I always had time to kill at the end of the day while she graded papers and prepared lesson plans. On a typical sunny Florida afternoon I went into my classroom through the propped-open door to play a game on the amazingly high tech classroom computer. We're talking something like Pong here, people. As in, "Bleep . . . (wait five minutes) . . . (return shot) Bleep . . ." I thought it was the coolest thing ever. I was the only one in the classroom, but being a teacher's kid came with privileges like peanut butter crackers and grape soda from the vending machine and access to classroom computers unsupervised. So I was allowed.

When it was time to head back to my mom's classroom, I shut the door behind me, causing it to lock automatically. In that moment, I realized I (gasp!) *left the computer on.* Now, remember, I was nine years old, and this was 1986, early tech days. I didn't understand very much about computers at all, but I was in awe of them and thought they had the power to blow up the world if you did one thing wrong. My mom still holds this view. *"Honey, I just touched something and it all disappeared! Oh no, oh mercy, where did it go? Space? I knew you should have never gotten me this thing!"*

I seriously thought that by not turning off the computer, I was ensuring it would explode within a matter of minutes. I have this perfectly crisp image of me running down the sidewalk, searching for my teacher, and feeling the horrible, unfamiliar sensation of my throat closing up. It was as if my windpipe had been shrunk down to the circumference of a coffee stirrer. Tears flowed down my cheeks as I fought for breath. *"The computer's going to blow up. The school is going to burn down. It will be all my fault."*

Thankfully, I found my teacher and she reassured me that computers can actually stay on for quite some time before they spontaneously combust. And that awful feeling in my throat? The result of a minor panic attack.

I was more fortunate than other children who have horror stories in their past. I honestly cannot remember another time I experienced this terrible feeling until the Passport Saga. Up until this point in the story, I knew things looked bleak, but I, and others in authority, believed that although we couldn't change the passport agent's mind, we could get an expedited Certificate of Citizenship (COC), and thus a passport. We had a United States Congressman and two U.S. Senators requesting the expedited COC, and we easily met the "extreme hardship" qualification. Seriously, all we needed was for someone to push "print."

At that point, we received a devastating blow. A congressional liaison at the Buffalo USCIS service center said that Lucy might not qualify for automatic citizenship. Although the passport agent had alluded to this, up until this point the people we spoke with in immigration or the State Department said that Lucy was, in fact, a U.S. citizen.

Now, immigration officials at the center that could actually give us the COC were questioning her citizenship. If Lucy didn't qualify for automatic citizenship, we would have to apply for her citizenship by filing a special application for naturalization, and this process could take up to *five or six months*. The longest I'd ever been away from my children was eight days. There was no way in the world I could be away from them, and my husband, for *five or six months!*

That feeling in my windpipe—the one I hadn't experienced in twenty-seven years—returned. My throat closed up. The walls seemed to be closing in, and there was no escape route in sight. Stress physically manifested itself in stomachaches and sleepless nights. All I could think about was the fact that my kids said good-bye to us on Christmas night with the understanding that they would see their new sister and me again in just two weeks, and I did not keep my end of the deal. I was a caged mama bear who couldn't get to her cubs. I was that nine-year-old girl again who felt responsible for a potential disaster, yet could do nothing about it. I was desperate.

January 14ᵗʰ, 2014

Have you ever been in a desperate situation? I mean like, stuck, see no way out, everything is out of your control, desperate? Before The Situation began two and a half weeks ago, I never had. Sure, I've walked through pain, deep pain, and it was awful. Yet, I've never felt desperate until now.

Maybe it's something about being the youngest child and having an older sister who always had my back. Except that time when she let me wear a homemade t-shirt to school the last day of fifth grade. I took one of my Dad's old Fruit of the Looms and wrote in big fat letters, with a black Sharpie, "School's Out." Except, I didn't judge the spacing well—I have a problem with depth perception—and it ended up looking like this: Schoo-

l's out!

Besides that, if there was a problem, yo, she'd solve it. She was my own personal Vanilla Ice. Or my Dad would come to my rescue. Or my friend Allison, who never does anything stupid or absent-minded, would bail me out. After marriage, Brian would answer my distress calls. I panic, they fix. Things would just work out.

Now, despite the amazing efforts of so many remarkable people, it's just not working out. In fact, it's getting worse. The blow we got today is the news that, at this point, there will be no expedited Certificate of Citizenship because USCIS is saying that it looks like Lucy did not meet the requirements for citizenship since she didn't come here to reside permanently. I'm not going to go into all the reasons why this is so incredibly wrong, but just trust me when I tell you, it is.

Today I was in the pit. Desperation overcame me and I could see no way out. "I can't breathe," I told my friend Allison as I sobbed on the phone. And I couldn't. "For the thing which I greatly feared is come upon me," Job said (Job 3:25). I agree.

I've never been here before. I've prayed for people in desperate situations, I've counseled people in desperate situations, but I have never been the one actually in the desperate situation, and now I am. I'm separated from the people I love the most. I'm not able to mother three of my children.

I am so sorry if I have ever trivialized the despair of someone who was in the dark and could see no way out, or if I have judged the way someone responded to a crushing situation. As a dear friend who battled terminal cancer told me, "You never

know how you're going to respond until you are in a situation."
Boy, is that ever true.

Now, some of you might think I seem a little unstable—full
of faith one day, in the pit the next, trusting and laughing the
next day, weeping the next, but isn't that what it really looks
like to walk by faith? From her lecture series, "Idol Addiction,"
Julie Sparkman says:

> *"Belief is not without fear, anger, darkness, disillusionment.*
> *"Belief does not mean I have to say these circumstances*
> *are good.*
> *"Belief is not a test of my competency or a test to prove my*
> *righteousness, defined by how well I respond to this. God uses*
> *bad and ugly but it doesn't make them right or okay. I am still*
> *in God's story of redemption—this chapter will not thwart that."*

Isn't that freeing? The Christian life is not a perfect tightrope
walk of always doing the right thing, saying the right thing,
never wavering. Instead, it's a wobbly procession of slipping
and stumbling, then refocusing your eyes on Jesus, walking
confidently, stumbling, refocusing, and walking again. It's our
humanity that reveals our need for Jesus and causes us to run
to Him again.

So, that's where I am. Today, I fell hard from the rope, but
thankfully landed on the comforting arms of Christ. Tomorrow,
we do battle again. Honestly, I don't feel up to it, but praise
God, He is.

Yes, I was a desperate woman riding a high-speed faith roller
coaster that I wished had been more like a steady monorail. Still,
being monorail-esque would not have been authentic to my tempera-
ment, nor to humanity in general, really. Through the incarnation of
Jesus, God showed us that emotions are not the enemy, but, instead,

an expression of His character. Just look at Jesus' reaction to the death of His friend Lazarus. He was grieving and sympathetic. He did not respond to the death of a friend, even one He knew He was going to raise from the dead, with stoic passivity. He *felt deeply,* and He wasn't ashamed for others to see Him feel. He saw His friends hurting and He hurt with them.

Walking through the heartache of human experiences gave Jesus empathy, for our sakes, so that we can know for a fact that we have a High Priest who sympathizes with our weaknesses. Walking through my own trial gave me a degree of empathy I did not have before for people who are stuck in despair. I can now weep for the adoptive mom whose son is stuck in the Congo because he can't get an exit visa. I have new insight into the dying mother's desire to do anything at all to be healed because she loves her children too much to leave them.

Instead of easily sweeping aside someone's doubts about God and His goodness with a pat theological answer, I can say, "Yeah, I doubt too." Before this particular tightrope walk of faith, I would respond too anxiously when Christians would confess they had doubts. I reminded them of things they already knew and perhaps glossed over their struggles to push them back on the path of Christian disciplines. I should have explored the depths of those doubts with them, trusting the One who will not let them go. I know better now.

I once heard that a death row inmate said, "Empathy doesn't say, 'That could be me.' Empathy says, 'That *is* me.'" Yes. This particular pain was opening my eyes to how much I was connected to others because, like them, I am a broken person in a broken world.

Back to that fateful day in the fourth grade, even though it was silly for me to think the school was going to blow up simply because I left the computer on, my teacher did not make me feel dumb, nor did she trivialize my response, which was clearly out of proportion with the situation. Similarly, I am grateful that even though God knows in the end, *it really will be okay,* that He is in control of our well being, and that He will make everything right, He never trivializes our pain. He doesn't call us "silly" or dismiss us because of our doubts. He is a safe place for us to say, "Lord I believe; help my unbelief" (Mark 9:24).

I would like to think this pain has changed me, and I will comfort others differently than I did before. I will not rush friends to the other side of challenging circumstances with quickly spouted verses. I won't judge someone's spirituality based on how quickly they can bounce back. Instead, I'll sit with others in their pain, in their desperation, and say, "You *are* me and your pain is my pain. Let's walk through all its intricacies and feel every part of it, and eventually we'll come out on the other side, but there is no rush. Take as long as you need."

I can't say I've always been a safe place for others' pain, but I pray that now, by God's grace, I am.

Chapter 16

How Long?

Just when we were about to give up hope on making a case for Lucy's right to automatic citizenship and file an application for citizenship instead, hope rose. Karla contacted a USCIS officer in Buffalo who had worked on another family's case and laid out the Lucy Situation. I also was able to plead personally for our case. I appealed the issue of precedence—hundreds of ex-pats before us easily obtained passports and citizenship for their adopted children. I reiterated our evidence of residence, showing that we were still heavily tied to the States. I pled the emotional side of our case: the crucial bonding time Lucy and Brian and the kids were missing, the medical care Lucy wasn't getting because our travel insurance didn't cover it, the agony of separation from the rest of the family.

Thankfully, the officer saw the urgency of our case and agreed to rebuild Lucy's file from the ground up and grant several congressmen's requests to expedite her case. We were finally seeing movement, finally talking to someone who actually could help us. Things were looking extremely promising for us to have a Certificate of Citizenship and a passport within a week! I began to pray in faith that this would be THE WEEK that Lucy and I would go home, and I asked others to pray.

School was about to start for the kids, and I couldn't fathom not being there. Brian had already done the "Back to School" preparations, per my instructions. "Check their shoes to see if they're still in good condition. Take them all for haircuts, but make sure the haircuts are subtle—not 'Look at me! It's the first day of school and I'm over-eager, so my bangs are only a millimeter long!'" I think you all would agree that this was crucial. "Deep clean their lunch boxes and their school bags, wash the uniforms, label the supplies . . ."

Even though it was a little bit of a vacation to escape some of these duties, especially the labeling of *every single crayon,* the Mom in me wanted to be the one to make sure they were ready for the new year. I wanted to snuggle with Sarah Kate the night before to calm any first day jitters. I wanted to be the one behind the camera for the mandatory first day of school pics on the driveway. I wanted to hold Sarah Kate's hand and walk her to her new class. I wanted to hear all about the day over homemade cookies. Sure, Brian could do all these things and do them well, but I just wanted to be there. I *needed* to be there. So we prayed.

But wait. Hadn't we prayed specifically towards a deadline before? That didn't go so well. Was it really wise to put my faith— and my kids' faith—on the line again?

January 20th, 2014

My parents tried to hide the fact that today was a holiday.

It might be a commentary on my mental and emotional state that they worried that I wouldn't be able to handle this news— that government agencies, namely USCIS, would be closed today and not working on THE most important case on their desk. (I'm sure I'm the only one who feels like her case is the most important.)

Brian accidentally spilled the beans to me on Saturday when we were Face Timing. He casually mentioned, "Yeah, it's extra disappointing that we didn't get any news on Friday, with the holiday on Monday and everything." Me: "Excuse me? There is no holiday on Monday." Brian: "Um, yes there is. MLKJr?"

I storm down the stairs. "What is this about Monday being a holiday?" Mom and Dad exchange nervous glances. "We didn't want to tell you." Well. That's love, isn't it? I'm just wondering how they intended to keep it a secret. "That's strange sweetheart, I guess everyone's super busy today and not answering their phones." I like to think I would catch on eventually, but it was kind of them to try.

The kids start a brand new school year a week from today. I can't tell you how much I want to be there. Sarah Kate wants me to braid her hair. Brian has been watching YouTube videos to learn how, but let's face it; she needs her mama to do it.

I realize that a couple of weeks ago, I asked people to pray in faith that we would get Lucy's passport by a certain deadline, the day of our scheduled flights. That didn't happen, and it was hard. So, there is part of me that hesitates in asking you to pray we'll be home in time for the kids' first day of school. What if it doesn't happen again?

I think even with the best of intentions, we can still tend to hold to some kind of superstitious approach to our prayers. Like, if I don't believe enough, God won't answer. What if I don't say the right thing? What if I still doubt? What if I'm not really sure what His will is, and I miss it? What if I'm wrong?

All of these thoughts have gone through my mind as I've been asking the Lord for this new deadline. My kids are praying for this deadline. What happens to their faith if the answer again is no? Then it struck me: God is my Father. Why do I think my communication with Him has to be perfect for Him to hear me?

I think about my own dad. I've been living at my parents' house for the last four weeks, and he has seen the good, the bad, and the ugly. He has seen me weep, get my hopes up, get disappointed, and weep again. He has seen me in victory and despair. Do you think he once has said, "Jennifer, you're not responding properly to this situation, so I'm not going to help you get Lucy a

passport. In fact, just don't talk to me about it anymore, okay?"
Absolutely not! Despite my oscillation between faithfulness and
faithlessness, he has not stopped loving me, providing for my
needs, and doing everything in his power to help me.

Why would it be any different with my Heavenly Father?
Prayer is messy. God isn't concerned with a formula; He just
wants to hear my heart.

During an interview following the release of Les Misera-
bles, Anne Hathaway discussed the nerves that gripped her when
she was preparing to sing the epic "I Dreamed a Dream." This
song seemed so iconic, and she was terrified that she would not
get it perfectly right. Sensing her anxiety, director Tom Hooper
took her aside and said, "It's not an iconic song. It's something
this woman is feeling and making sense of, and it's a howl."
Meaning, sing it as a guttural cry of the soul. And boy did she
ever, giving a raw, Oscar-winning performance that won't easily
be forgotten.[6]

Prayer is not neat and pretty. In fact, it can be downright
ugly. It's a baring of our souls before the Lord, a combination of
crying out to Him, thanking Him, doubting, being reminded
of Truth, and crying out to Him again. It's a howl.

So here's my howl tonight: "God, I want to go home to my
husband and my children. It's hard to pray this, because I've
been disappointed before. But, I want to be there on their first
day of school to pack their lunches and iron their uniforms and
braid my baby girl's hair. I'm ready to hold them again."

Please join me in praying that God will make a way for
me to go home this week. Pray for a kind woman in immigration who has graciously chosen to review our case. And praise
Him for being a God who encourages us to cast our cares on
Him, because He cares for us (1 Peter 5:7).

So, we prayed, in faith, trusting God for big things. The kids continued to mark off days on the ongoing "Mom and Lucy Coming Home Calendar," in anticipation that The Day would come soon. On Wednesday January 22nd, the Buffalo USCIS processing center informed us that a decision had been made regarding Lucy's citizenship, but, "due to the unique circumstances," it would be reviewed by a supervisor, and the final answer would be given the next day.

Friends in Brisbane said, "See you at school next week!" American friends said, "Eat as much Chick-fil-A as you can these next few days, because you won't have another opportunity for a long time!" *Everyone,* including Brian and me, just knew the answer would be yes. I started scouting out plane tickets for the coming weekend, eyeballing ridiculously expensive fares, but who cares? We believed we were going home! Surely this was the miracle we'd been praying for!

Thursday came. I waited by my phone, my sister by my side, sweet tea in hand and ready to celebrate. Mid-afternoon the email arrived.

It was a no.

Lucy's automatic citizenship was officially denied because they claimed we did not meet the permanent residency requirement—a requirement we didn't even know existed before this drama began. We learned that there were two parts to the Child Citizenship Act of 2000. Adopted children who come to America to reside permanently qualify for automatic citizenship under one section; adopted children who are not permanently residing in the States have to apply for citizenship, under a different section.

Apparently, before us, most passport offices and USCIS had either granted ex-pat families the residency requirement, or didn't really know about the requirement, so the issue was hardly ever raised. Our case just happened to be one of the few that were flagged, causing us to be, to my knowledge, the first adoptive family to be separated because our child's citizenship was denied.

Lucy and I would not be going home. I would not be there for my kids' first day of school. I was staring into the reality that it could take months to resolve this matter—months of separation from my husband and three older children. These were crucial months of Lucy's development and attachment that Brian and the other kids could never get back.

Exhausting, lonely months of raising an internationally adopted child alone.

I crumbled. I picked up the phone and, through broken sobs, told Brian the news that I desperately wanted to reverse. Our family would remain separated with no end in sight.

January 23, 2014

Home felt so close I could almost taste it.

In my imagination, I could see my kids' huge grins as I rounded the corner at the airport and spotted them for the first time. I could feel my little girl's curls tickling my nose as I buried my face in her hair. I could hear my sons arguing about how much Lucy had REALLY grown since they saw her last. I could feel my husband's warm, strong embrace. I could envision the tears in his eyes as he held his baby girl for the first time in over a month and gently kissed her nose.

So close. So very, very close.

It reminds me of the half marathon I ran a few years ago. This was my second half marathon, and I was so excited. My training had gone really well, my iPod was loaded with all my favorite tunes, and I was pumped to be running with my friend Jenny. It was going to be a fantastic race.

Except three miles in, I knew something was wrong. My legs felt heavy, my skin felt clammy, and my breathing was way off. At five miles, a distance that was easy for me, I was considering quitting. I felt that bad. What I found out later was a major blood sugar dip was causing my body to be all out of whack. I pushed myself mile after mile, feeling sicker with each step, and was relieved when I was running what I thought was the last mile. As horrible as it had been, it was about to be over. The end was in sight.

So I thought.

Then I saw the sign that said I had one more mile to go. This is the point that my body said, "No more," and I started to black out and stagger.

This whole mess with Lucy's passport and citizenship has felt the same way. I started out feeling well prepared. We had researched, filled out all the paperwork correctly, and knew things should go without a hitch. Then it became obvious that something was wrong, and I've been staggering, wounded, towards the finish line ever since.

This week I thought the end was in sight. I truly believed that I was just a few days from jumping on a plane that would take Lucy and me to the rest of our family, and this would all be behind us.

Today, I found out the race isn't over yet. Instead of the sign saying, "One more mile," it's more like, "Keep running until we tell you to stop, and we're not really sure when that will be. So good luck with that."

I am so very tired. Tired of forms and requirements and deadlines and expectations and disappointments. Tired of hearing my little girl ask, "Good news?" only to have to say, "No baby, not today."

The most-asked question in the Bible is, "How long?" I can understand why.

In the midst of all this confusion and anguish, I witnessed a miracle last night. Lucy was fussing at bedtime, which is unusual for her. I sat down with her in the rocking chair and thought, "Let's just see." She has never let me rock her with her facing me.

She usually pushes me away, and I end up sitting her in my lap facing outwards. Last night, I thought I'd give it another try.

At first, it was just as I predicted. She pushed me away and kept her body perfectly straight. Even though her eyes were heavy, she refused to lay her head down. Then, it happened. Cautiously at first, she dipped her head towards my shoulder. Back up it went. Then again, with a little more trust this time, she laid down her head, just as my other three so naturally had done as babies.

I held my breath, not wanting to startle her in any way. Her body relaxed, melted onto mine, and she slept.

Today, I see so much of myself in Lucy. I do not like this path God has our family on. I push Him away and demand another way. I'm tempted to say, "You are not good." But then His character beckons me—His faithfulness, His love, and His promises to never leave me or forsake me and to always work all things together for my good and His glory. He calls me to unclench my fists, to lean in towards Him, and to rest.

I'm like Lucy. I tentatively lean in, and then I push away again, but He gently reminds me again of this truth: It is not in good news or met deadlines and expectations that I'll find relief; it's in His embrace.

I pray for the grace to believe that truth and stay, resting in Him, for as long as it takes.

Oh, and about that race? Do you want to know how I got to the finish line? A stranger saw me stumbling and came out of the crowd to my aid. When I insisted I didn't want to go to the medic but wanted to finish the race, she actually held me up and walked me through that last mile.

Brian and I have felt held up by so many of you during this journey. I don't know how long this "last leg" will be, but we cannot do it alone. Keep holding us up, friends—all the way to the finish line.

We were held up indeed. When I posted the news that immigration had given us a no, All Things Communication went crazy with an incessant pinging of indignation, Scripture, inspirational quotes, and good old-fashioned love.

I just have to share some of those soul-soothing messages:

"We know that God has the power to make all things right. He has the might to work this miracle that you need. While we don't know when He will, we absolutely know He is able! And in that we can rest, because He promises us that He hears our prayers and will meet our needs. God is able to deliver! My faith and prayer life have been multiplied during these past few weeks as I have brought your needs before the Lord. The fact that the Holy Spirit is interceding for us when we don't have the words anymore to pray has brought me peace."

"There is nothing I can say to ease or abate your groaning to return and reunite your family. The Lord is with you and He is working for His name's sake, strengthening your weak arms and feeble knees by confessing your disappointment, confessing your weakness, anger, anguish and doubt. Cry out to the One who has saved us from the consequences of our sin, bought us out of a destiny of a lake of sulfur and fire and into a home filled with many rooms, a feast and a throne. There are clouds of witnesses above and around you urging you on. They, too, have suffered and overcome and are now reaping their rewards. Consider them, consider Christ who also had just 'one more mile to go' when beaten and bloodied, then had to drag His cross uphill and be nailed to it before 'It was finished.' For the joy set before Him, He endured the cross, scorning its shame. Keep going Jen."

And perhaps the one that pierced my heart the most:

"Sweet Jennifer, you are not forgotten."

My friend Lisa walks intimately with Jesus, and I know He gave her those words at just the right time, a time when the Scripture I identified most with was, "My tears have been my meat day and night, while they continually say to me, Where is your God?" (Psalms 42:3). Except it wasn't people who were saying this to me, it was the Enemy, whispering lies like, "Either God doesn't see you, or He doesn't care." Either option was hopeless and debilitating.

Then came Lisa's reminder: "*You are not forgotten,*" and I wept huge, relieved tears.

What hope! God had not forgotten me; actually, He was still very much involved in this story with all its twists and turns. He would redeem the lost time, and "though He slay me" (Job 13:15), I could still praise Him, because the anguish was creating in me a broken, beautiful offering, the very opposite of a whitewashed tomb.

A broken offering. Isn't that what I really want to be?

Chapter 17

Stuck While I'm Stuck

There's a saying about "adding insult to injury."

Here's an example: In the sixth grade, not only did I make the fashion mistake of wearing turquoise, elastic-waistband pants to school, but I accidentally wore them *backwards.* I only discovered this when I went to put my hands in my pockets and thought, "Hey, wait a second—"

And another one: Not only did my friend Jen and I get zero sleep the last night of high school church camp because we stayed up all night on the beach lamenting our ex-boyfriends, but on the bus ride home, our friends raised our Dramamine-induced comatose arms, volunteering us to stick around for *forty-eight more hours* while we waited for one of the buses to be fixed. I still haven't forgiven them for that. Especially since afore-mentioned ex-boyfriends stayed around too, with their newfound loves. That was fun.

Hey, how about this one?

Not only were Lucy and I indefinitely stuck a bazillion miles away from the rest of our family, but I actually got stuck while I was stuck due to the Snowpocalypse of 2014.

I can't make this stuff up, folks.

I was obviously beyond sad about Lucy's citizenship being denied and downright depressed about missing the kids' first day of school. One of my best friends encouraged me to come and visit her in Birmingham for a few days. She thought a change of scenery would help get my mind off The Situation. Fair enough. Plus, there would be some serious eating out involved.

I was sold. What else was I going to do? My dad hired an immigration attorney who helped us file an application for naturalized citizenship. Congressional requests had once again been submitted for the case to be expedited. If their requests were granted, things could be resolved in a matter of weeks. If it wasn't granted, the wait would be a minimum of five months. So really, all there was for me to do at this point was to wait, pray, and lament. I could lament at my parents' house, where we had been holed up for the past six weeks, or I could lament with my face in a bowl of chicken waldorf salad with my best friends. I chose the latter.

Here was the plan: Drive to Birmingham, spend two nights at Allison's house, do mindless things like stroll the Galleria and eat Gigi's cupcakes, and then return to my parents' house to resume the immigration battle.

Things didn't quite pan out the way I'd envisioned. I'm starting to see a theme here, Lord.

February 1, 2014

"Come to Birmingham," she said. "You need a break from the stress. It will be good for you to get out of the house."

Famous last words.

I took my friend's advice. (And by the way, I totally don't blame her—I just wanted to get a reaction out of her when she reads this. You're allowed to do that when you've been friends for almost twenty years.)

Lucy and I drove to Birmingham on Sunday afternoon. It was a beautiful day, with minimal fussing from Lucy. I enjoyed seeing my in-laws and adorable niece that evening, and arrived at Jay and Allison's house that night.

The next day was great—just what the doctor ordered. Lunch at California Pizza Kitchen, and a group of my closest friends came over that night to distract me from the painfully obvious: It was the kids' first day of school in Australia, and I wasn't there.

Brian packed the lunches, ironed the uniforms, braided Sarah Kate's hair—extremely well, I might add—held Sarah Kate's hand, and walked them into school. I still can't believe I wasn't there. My heart hurt so much this day that I thought it would burst. So, what did my friends do?

As it says in Ecclesiastes, there's a time for everything: a time to laugh, a time to cry, a time to mourn, and a time to DANCE. That's right—Just Dance on the Wii, baby! I do have a picture of this, but certain members of this group made us practically swear with blood that no one would post them.

We ate chocolate cake and danced it up to "Proud Mary," among other things. It was balm to my soul, I tell you. There are probably few people who have prayed for my family and me more than these five women, but these girls know me, and they knew on this night, the best way to cheer me up was to get my groove on.

When we could dance no more, everyone parted ways. "See you at lunch tomorrow!" What is that line about "the best laid plans of mice and men?"

Around nine-thirty the next morning, the snow started to fall. "Aw, bummer," I said to Allison. "Do you think we'll have to cancel lunch?" "Nah, we're only supposed to get a dusting." Then school was cancelled, and Snowmageddon, the Snowpocalypse,

Winter Gridlock 2014—take your pick of cheesy labels (because we have to label everything)—began.

Lucy and I were supposed to go back to Memphis that day. Instead, we ended up stranded.

My two "stress-free" days turned into six days and a dose of cabin fever. Although there were fun moments in the snow, honestly, it was all pretty painful for me. Every time I heard a story about someone stuck, trying to get to her kids, every time I heard the panic, the pain, in a mother's voice as she documented her account of sitting for hours on a highway-turned-parking lot, fighting to reunite with her children who were stranded elsewhere, all I could think was, "This is my life."

I feel like I've been stranded on I-65 for six weeks now, creeping along at a snail's pace, desperate to get to my husband and children, but I can't. Let me tell you, I've tried every path possible. I've tried walking, running, snowboarding, hitching rides, phoning friends, four-wheeling, all to no avail.

I'm still waiting on my reunion picture.

Today is the first of February. I last saw my husband and children on Christmas night. It has been a long, hard, frustrating road. I cannot believe we're still here. It's like that scene in The Croods *where they all jump out of the giant popcorn and say, "Still alive!" But instead, I'm like, "Still here!" and it's not a good thing.*

For those of you who don't know, towards the end of January 2014, what was supposed to be a light dusting turned heavy snow on already cold streets, which turned into skating rinks in a matter of minutes. Unsuspecting motorists began slipping, sliding, careening, and colliding. In the blink of an eye, roads became undrivable. Kids were stuck at school because their parents couldn't get to them, employees were forced to sleep at their desks, and thousands spent the night on the interstate, in the bitter cold. Roads weren't safe for four days, which meant Lucy and I had to stay put.

Okay. Let's be honest. Was it really a *terrible* thing that I spent six days in Birmingham instead of two? I mean, thankfully, Lucy and I didn't try to go home the morning the snow began to fall, so we were stuck in a warm house instead of on a cold highway, but it was just the *principle* of the matter. I already felt trapped and helpless, and the fact that yet again, I was trying to leave one place to go to another and couldn't was just ridiculous. How dare my plans be thwarted once again!

Then I started reading desperate Facebook pleas from mamas trying to get to their babies across town. Hundreds of posts went something like this:

"Been trying to get to my kids' school for the last four hours!"

"My kids are going to have to spend the night across town. I did everything possible to get to them but nothing worked."

"Anyone have a four wheeler I can borrow to get to my kid?"

I felt for them, I really did, but truth be told, I was jealous. My panicked frenzy, my longing to be reunited with my family was entering its seventh week. Unlike these other desperate mamas, my situation was not resolved within forty-eight hours, and I was mad about it. I couldn't stomach any more dramatic snow reunion pics because they were reminders that I didn't have my own.

Typical, huh?

We find it hard to rejoice when others rejoice when we can't get past our own disappointments. It is hard to cheer for the "haves" when we are the "have nots."

Comparison can be excruciating. The single woman wears bridesmaid dress after ugly bridesmaid dress, smiling for the camera, yet imploring the Lord, "Do You not see me?" The bereaved mother weeps silently through yet another baby dedication. The beaten-down, unemployed father is passed up for a job offer, again.

I learned two major things while in my "nightmare within the nightmare":

First of all, when I am one of the "haves," I want to be aware of the "have nots." How can I be sensitive to that single friend, to that woman who desperately wants to be a mother? How can I enter into her world without being a constant reminder of her disappointments? How can my conversations with her be others-centered? How can I gently love?

Secondly, the Bible commands us to rejoice when others rejoice, so that must mean through the power of the Holy Spirit, it is possible. Withholding joy from others doesn't change my own circumstances, it merely breeds bitterness, and bitterness poisons my heart.

Does this mean I ignore my pain or deny it exists? No. Not possible. Yet, something special about Jesus shines when, through tears of longing, we can genuinely say, "I'm happy for you."

A friend whose husband had been out of work for months followed Lucy's story closely. When we eventually got good news about Lucy's citizenship, she sent this encouragement:

"Rejoicing with you today that you are finally getting to go home! We are still waiting, but your answered prayer gives us hope."

I may as well have been standing on holy ground. Only God's redeeming grace can enable that kind of response. May the answered prayers of others give us not discouragement about what we lack, but hope that in His timing, in His understanding, in His perfect ways, He will give us everything we need.

Chapter 18

The Transforming Power of Love

think I've made it clear that I am resistant to change. Whether that's change in life circumstances, plans, fashion, technology, or my own heart, I'm not for it, at least initially.

When I was a high school sophomore, one Sunday evening we were loading up to go to church, or so I thought. Somehow I missed the memo that we were actually driving an hour and a half to see some relatives for the evening. I lost it. Had an absolute conniption.

"What do you mean we're going to Dyersburg? I can't go to Dyersburg! I wasn't planning on going to Dyersburg! I thought we were going to church!"

I think my parents thought I was having a nervous breakdown, and perhaps an unplanned trip to small town Tennessee would push me over the edge, because they actually turned the car around and dropped me back off at home. They were much more gracious than I think I'd be to my own kids if they ever pulled something like that. I would be more like, "Get over it, Drama Queen; we're going to Dyersburg."

The point is, there was nothing wrong with Dyersburg; it just wasn't my plan for the night. I'm pretty sure my plan involved going to church and seeing the boy I had a crush on. Shouldn't have given in, Mom and Dad.

Through many sanctifying years, Brian has learned not to spring change on me. Instead of throwing me into the boiling pot of Change of Direction, he knows I need to sit in the comfortable room temperature water of My Own Plans while the Dial of Modification is gradually turned up. *Do I really need to rehash the five-year-long saga of us deciding to move overseas?*

Seven weeks into Operation Passport, my flailing temper tantrum was finally subsiding, and I began to consider what the Lord was doing here. Yes, He was doing a work in me; He always does when trouble abounds. Yet there was another little person stuck right alongside me. What was God doing in her?

Before, all I could think about were the negative effects of Lucy being separated from the rest of her new family and from medical care covered by insurance. I could only see the missed vital days of cocooning in her permanent home with her permanent family. Let me be clear, these were very serious concerns, but if God works all things for our good and His glory, then it means when Lucy's passport application was denied, He had her good in mind as well.

A timely email was the decisive blow in breaking my defenses. With new eyes, I could see that our unwanted change of plans was actually God's gift to His tiny little child.

February 4, 2014

It's amazing how God uses different people at different times to tell you exactly what you need to hear.

Over the past six weeks, I've received Scripture, YouTube videos, inspirational songs, personal stories, empathy, and compassion, all at just the right times. There have been many moments when I thought, "I can't do this another minute," and I'd look in my inbox to see a message, "Wanted you to know that I'm thinking about you." I would find strength to go another step.

This week, an email from a friend casually referred to "this gift of (my) time in the U.S." Hmmm. Gift? Really? Because usually, those are fun to receive, except that time that Brian re-gifted to me a gift I had previously given to him. Oh, wait; have I shared that story before? I digress.

"This gift of my time in the U.S."

That perspective is a difficult one to fight for, but it's right. If I'm God's child, and He desires to give His children good gifts, then there are elements of this ongoing detour to be celebrated, the main one being Lucy's transformation.

When Lucy became ours on December 16th, we were shocked by her lack of development, teensy tiny size, and sensory issues. Any kind of stimulation overwhelmed her, and she preferred to be alone in her bed. She hated to be touched. She couldn't roll over or sit up, couldn't easily grasp objects, and rejected any form of food besides her bottle.

It has been a gift indeed to be able to pour myself into Little Lucy. The name of the game has been Patient Pursuit. This reality applies to all aspects of being her mother, from teaching her to eat to earning the privilege of her affection.

In seven weeks' time, Lucy has gone from a helpless infant who could only lie on her back and play with her hands, and didn't know how to eat, to a happy, interactive delight who crawls like a champ, plays peek-a-boo and pat-a-cake, says "Uh oh" when she drops something, eats a container of baby food per sitting, and climbs into my lap for comfort, just to name a few accomplishments.

Lucy is sixteen months old. Developmentally, she was a five month old when we got her. In seven weeks, she's progressed to the stage of a nine to twelve month old. Unbelievable!

Now, it would have been silly for Brian and me to demand that she catch up developmentally and physically before we adopted her. Ludicrous, right? Because there was no way that she was going to get there on her own, in her crib unattended for most hours of the day. She had nothing to offer us, but we couldn't wait to give her all that was ours, and love her towards her utmost potential.

Yet, she still has a long way to go. Do I say, "Well Lucy, it's great that you're eating stage one baby foods, but your cousin who is two months younger than you is eating pepperoni pizza, so you need to step it up"? Of course not. Instead, I celebrate baby steps. I celebrated when she let me rub her mouth with a cloth without screaming. I celebrated when she could look at a spoon and not freak out. I threw a ridiculous looking party the first time applesauce entered her mouth and she actually closed her mouth and swallowed.

I celebrate these milestones with the end in mind. I know that one day Lucy will eat table food like a normal toddler. Because I know what she was created to be and do, I can cheer her on as she journeys towards that goal.

Surely we can't miss the parallels here.

God does not ask us to get our acts together before He adopts us as His children. We're simply incapable without the transforming power of His love. We have nothing to offer Him, yet everything that is His becomes ours.

When God looks at us, He has the end in mind. He knows what we were created to be and do, and He cheers us on as we take baby steps towards that goal. He doesn't throw His hands up in frustration when we don't master perfection, because He knows we're not there yet. He rejoices in our victories and shows compassion in our failures.

His is a Patient Pursuit.

Oh, what love can do! I've seen it in my own heart as God continues to change me to be more and more like Him, even though it is painful at times. I see it in Lucy every day, not only as she thrives physically, but as she learns to give and receive love.

Would this have still happened if we had gotten Lucy's passport and gone home as scheduled? Probably, in due time. Maybe this "gift of time in the U.S." has been about my needing to slow down to lavish this little girl with my undivided affection, to fill up in her what has been lacking all her life. And for me to stand in wonder once again at God's transforming power of love.

Lucy and I weren't the only ones being transformed. The winds of change were blowing across our whole family, and pain begat fruits of the spirit that grow best in the soil of suffering. With tears I wrote this letter to my older three:

Dear Joshua, Andrew, and Sarah Kate,
How can I begin to describe how very proud I am of you?

From the time Dad and I sat you down to tell you we were thinking about adopting, the three of you have been on board. You were sad for the baby girls in China who were abandoned daily, and you agreed we should bring one of them home. Sarah Kate, you were ecstatic with joy at the thought of finally being a big sister. You jumped up and down and squealed!

It was a long road to get to Lucy. Lots of paperwork, lots of time Dad and I had to spend on the phone and the computer to move on to the next step. A year went by, but you all were just as excited.

I'll never forget that day in the park when we told you we had been matched with Lucy. We showed you her picture and you couldn't get over how cute she was. You wanted to look at her videos over and over again. There were no doubts in your minds; she was your sister.

Sarah Kate, you were the best at counting down our steps to traveling to China. You had them memorized, so when we passed one step you knew exactly which one was coming next.

You helped me completely clean out your room from top to bottom and redesign the room to fit two. You even cleaned the windowsills, because you wanted everything "super clean for Lucy." You filled Lucy's crib with your stuffed animals.

When the time came to go, none of you complained that two weeks of your meager six weeks' summer vacation would be spent in China, in the cold. From the moment they placed Lucy in my arms, you each loved her as your own. You never complained about her constant crying, or the long waits at government agencies. You were rock stars.

When Lucy and I said good-bye to you at the Guangzhou airport, you were so brave. Even though you were sad to be separated from us, you knew it wouldn't be for long, and you were looking forward to some fun time with Dad. You said, "I love you Mom. See you in two weeks."

We all know that two weeks has turned into seven weeks and counting. It hasn't been easy on any of us. You miss me, you miss Lucy, and you miss our family being together. Thank God for Face Time, but it just isn't the same, is it?

Andrew, I can kiss as close to my screen as I can get, but I won't land on your chubby cheek. Sarah Kate, even though you take the iPad up to your bed so we can "snuggle," I know it's not the same thing as me wrapping my arms around you and singing as you fall asleep. Joshua, we can still talk through the challenges of your day, but it's not the same as going to my room, closing the door, and me scratching your back as we have one of our little chats.

It would be very understandable for you all to be resentful of this adoption, resentful of Lucy. After all, before December 16th, we were doing great as a family. You are at ages where we can do some really fun things together. We would have spent the last seven weeks swimming, going to the beach, going to the movies, playing games, and just being together.

Instead, I'm half a world away, caring for a baby that you've only known for less than two months.

Not once have you resented her.

Instead, you beg to see her when we Face Time, and you laugh at her latest tricks. You giggle when she stands on her head, you celebrate when she crawls, and you egg her on when she spits out her baby food all over the place. (Seriously, you have to stop doing that.)

You have never said, "If only we hadn't adopted her."

My, what character you have shown.

You are learning so much right now, you don't even realize it yet—things that will strengthen you and build a solid foundation for you to stand on in life. You are learning the true, painful cost of considering someone more than yourself, of laying aside your rights and privileges for the sake of another. You're learning that in order to love someone, you must sacrifice.

You're learning that God doesn't always answer our prayers the way we want Him to, but that doesn't mean we stop praying, and it doesn't mean He isn't real. You're learning that His ways are higher than our ways, and sometimes He asks us to do things that are just plain hard, and we may never know why. You're learning that it's okay to tell God you're mad at Him and you don't like His plan, because He wants to hear your heart, and He loves you anyway.

You're experiencing firsthand the grace He gives us in the midst of suffering, and you're seeing that He physically shows us His grace through others acting as the hands and feet of Jesus. Hopefully in turn, one day you will be the hands and feet of Jesus to others. By walking through pain, you will be more able to show compassion to others who are hurting.

You are gaining a richness and depth to your faith that is unusual for ones so young. I pray that this will help you face future trials, and we know that more trials will come. You are being equipped for those now.

How I wish I could snap my fingers and be home with you this very minute. As we wait, remember, "For our light affliction, which is but for a moment, works for us a far more exceeding and eternal weight of glory" (2 Corinthians 4:17).

I could not be more proud of you. Lucy is so blessed to be your "mei-mei" (little sister).

Once when I asked my friend Jackie what God was doing in her life, she responded, "Jennifer, God loves me so much that He won't leave me as I am. Because He loves me, He uses painful things to make me more like Him."

This "gift of time in the U.S." This gift of pain.

Lord, let me always have eyes to see my circumstances in such a radical way.

Chapter 19

We're Outta Here!

*A*s thankful as I was for the lessons God was teaching us all through this season of trial and separation, the fact still remained: We needed to get home. In a desperate moment when I could not take another day of "no news," of hearing the clock chime five and knowing another work day had come and gone without progress made, I wrote this to our lawyer:

> *When you call for an update tomorrow, please convey the crucial need for this to go quickly. Tomorrow I am having my first required post-adoption visit by a social worker. This was supposed to have been done in Australia, and the requirement is that both spouses be present. The CCWA is allowing an exception due to the extreme circumstances, but it still isn't right. I had to compile pictures of Lucy's first month "home." Brian is obviously not in any of them, and we aren't even home yet.*
>
> *Lucy is missing out on vital immunizations, testing, frequent observation by a pediatrician, and physical therapy because we cannot pay for these things out of pocket here in the U.S., whereas she will automatically be added to our insurance once we get to Australia.*
>
> *She has missed out on six crucial weeks of bonding with Brian and our other children. She thinks my parents are part*

of her nuclear family, and that their home is her home. She is going to regress when we get back, and this will increase in severity the longer we wait.

Above all of this, I have missed six weeks of my children's lives already. My husband is juggling a job and full-time parenting with no family close by. You cannot imagine how difficult it is to hear your six-year-old daughter cry every day and say, "I need you Mommy. Please come home."

I am not trying to be dramatic here—just again, painting the severe nature of this situation. We need to go home. I realize things take time, but we have been led down rabbit trails for six weeks already, and it is past time for this to be made right.

My lawyer very kindly told me to simmer down and let her work her magic.

One week later, a break appeared in the clouds. Light! After two months of hearing "no," just like that, as if it were the easiest thing in the world, the "yeses" rushed in. Say what?

February 14, 2014

We're bustin' this joint. Flying the coop. Peacin' out. SEE-ya!

After TWO MONTHS of waiting, pleading, and chasing rabbit trails that ended up being dead ends, the dam finally broke this week and the good news started pouring in. This is how it went down:

Monday: *Email from immigration saying that they decided to expedite Lucy's application for citizenship, meaning we would by-pass the five-month wait. Although we were relieved, we still didn't know quite what that meant time-wise. We've also had her case expedited once before, only to get "no" as the final decision, so we were only cautiously optimistic.*

Tuesday: The USCIS supervisor called me and asked if we could come in at nine the next morning for Lucy's citizenship interview. I said, "Nah, I was planning on eating breakfast at Chick-fil-A and then watching 'Let's Make A Deal, Valentine's Week.'"

Um, no. I said, "Of course! We'll be there!" I hung up the phone and shrieked in excitement.

Wednesday: We drove through icy roads and traffic jams to arrive at the interview with only a few minutes to spare (because this story can never be without drama). After reviewing Lucy's file, the supervisor said, "Okay, we'll go ahead and print the certificate." Seriously? That's it?? A short time later, she handed me the proverbial golden ticket, declared Lucy an American citizen, and I almost kissed her on the face. Almost.

I immediately called the passport office—where this mess began—and told them we had the certificate. The Senator's office had already been in contact with them that day, strongly urging them to process the passport quickly, so they were ready for us.

She gave us an appointment time of 8:00 a.m. Thursday. Dad, Lucy, and I loaded up and headed to the passport agency for the third time in seven weeks (each time in hope of returning with a passport). We chowed on some Cracker Barrel biscuits, called the Comfort Inn home for the night, and prayed for this all finally to come to an end the next morning.

Thursday: Showed up at the passport agency at 8:00 sharp, presented the certificate, and was given a passport by 9:15. Tears filled my eyes as the agent handed me Lucy's passport. I couldn't believe it. That little blue book that we, and so many others, had prayed for, cried over, stressed over for two months was actually in my hands. We were free to go home!! No. Way.

We're seriously going home. Tomorrow. I still can't believe it.

We were going home. It was really happening! Lucy's new passport might as well have been a check from Publishers Clearing House, because I felt like the richest woman in the world. Gates that had been stubbornly, senselessly sealed shut for two months were suddenly unhinged and flung open wide, and Lucy and I were free to race through to the four most important people in our lives. My own personal Berlin Wall had been smashed to smithereens. *We were going home.*

After two months of what felt like inactivity, the Green Light felt so sudden, it didn't feel real. Kind of like a World Cup soccer game that goes zero-zero for eighty-nine minutes and fifty-nine seconds, and lo and behold, a star striker fires one past the goalie in that final second to win the game. For a few pulses in time, everyone is almost too stunned to celebrate.

That was me. I had unsuccessfully pled for the Magical Documents for what felt like the longest, most horrible game ever, and in the final second, before the game was forced into quadruple overtime, those powerful papers were in my hand. So elated, so stunned. So thankful.

God bless the Internet. I was incredibly grateful to so many people, and was able to thank thousands at the same time. Maybe technology isn't so bad after all?

February 14, 2014

There are so many people I want to thank, and there's no way I'll cover everyone in this short space, so even if I don't mention you by name, please know that I am so grateful for how everyone has blessed our family these last few months. Huge thanks to . . .

. . . my parents, who graciously welcomed me and Lucy into their quiet lives for two months, feeding and sheltering us,

and going to battle with me each day to get us home. They saw the ugliest sides of me during this ordeal and loved me anyway. Thank you for literally sparing no expense to see my family reunited. I love you. Thank you to my sister for keeping me sane in ways that only a sister can.

. . . my in-laws and extended family for caring for us with your prayers, visits, financial help, and the list goes on. Thank you Richard for dropping everything you were doing multiple times to help me with documents and phone calls, not only because I was crying and begging you to, but because you wanted to. Thank you Aunt Donna for driving two-and-a-half hours to see me on a freezing cold night because I received a "no" from immigration, and you knew I was devastated.

. . . my Lifeline social worker Karla, who literally bore this burden as if it were her own. I can't count the number of nights that she and I emailed back and forth at midnight, brainstorming action plans and sharing encouraging words. She contacted me every single day of this nightmare and did not rest until it was resolved. Karla, as we've said, we are bonded for life. You loved my family so well through this entire process. I love you friend.

. . . Congressman Bachus, Senator Corker, Senator Alexander, and their corresponding aides Christian, Stephanie, and Mary. They worked countless hours on our behalf and played huge roles in finally getting this all resolved. Thank you, Christian, for speaking truth to me right when I needed it. Thank you, Stephanie, for promising me that, no matter what any other office did, you would not stop working on our behalf until we made it back home. Thank you Mary, for responding to my tears with tenderness.

. . . Allison, for hosting Lucy and me so graciously two different times—one longer than the other, thanks to the Snowpocalypse! Thank you for loving my high maintenance, dramatic self,

*and praying us back home. Thank you to all my other precious
friends around the world—literally!—for regularly checking in
on me, sending encouragement my way, and praying so faithfully. I read every single word and my burden was lightened.*

*. . . my Christ Community family for supporting me with
your words, and for upholding my family with your physical acts
of grace and care. What an awesome community with which we
have the privilege of worshiping! Thank you Chapel Hill friends
for serving Brian and the kids with play dates, transportation,
and meals. Thank you Catherine for clarifying to Brian that
when you said Sarah Kate needed a "hair clip," that did not
mean he needed to cut her hair!!*

*. . . my incredible husband Brian, for carrying a load
beneath which most men would have crumbled. You have been
a rock for the kids and me. There aren't enough words to say
how grateful I am for you. Thank you Joshua, Andrew, and
Sarah Kate, for displaying such patience and strength, and for
enduring Dad's cooking.*

*. . . Jesus, for carrying me through the toughest storm of my
life. Thank You for proving Yourself to be faithful, even though
Your time frame did not match mine. Although I wouldn't have
chosen this road, I am so grateful for the rich lessons You taught
me along the way, the "treasures of darkness, and hidden riches
of secret places" (Isaiah 45:3). Thank You for meeting me in the
dark many nights at three a.m. as I cried out to You, begging
You to show Your face. Thank you for hearing my accusations
that You either didn't see me or You didn't care, and for loving
me back to the truth. Thank You for patiently pursuing me even
when I was questioning everything I believed about You. You
are real, and You are worthy.*

*. . . YOU—Readers, in the thousands, who have followed
our story. So many of you don't even know us, yet wept over
our heartache. Thank you for journeying with us, and as my*

*friend Natalie said, "storming the gates" on our behalf. I am
so humbled and grateful.*

And just like that, in God's perfect timing birthed out of a
wisdom that far surpasses my own, we were homeward bound.

Chapter 20

Finally Home

THE DAY. It finally came! Hope morphed into reality. The deepest cries of my heart were being fulfilled. Lucy and I were at the airport yet again, this time headed towards *home*.

Can elation and deep sorrow coexist? I believe they did at the Delta terminal that day. To go towards something you must leave something behind, and in this case, it meant my father. My mom was traveling with me, and even though I had to say good-bye to my sister and her family, they had plans to visit within six months. The earliest I would see my Dad again was two years. *Two years.*

He snuggled Lucy on his lap like a good Papaw should, kissing her cheek and singing his special Chinese lullaby meant only for her. Then it was my turn. If only a bear hug could have adequately communicated the appreciation I felt for all he had done to see my family reunited—the hours on the road, the phone calls to Congressmen, the days of work missed, the prayers prayed in late and early hours, the words of encouragement to press on. If only all adoptive families could experience the adoration and acceptance he lavished on Lucy from the moment he laid eyes on her. No doubt, she was his granddaughter, and he was her Papaw. My heart could have burst with gratitude.

I squeezed him tight and said, "See you soon," even though we both knew it wasn't true. My heart was heavy with the grief that accompanies good-byes, yet free at the same time, because I knew what awaited me on the other side of world. The plane couldn't possibly fly fast enough.

February 17, 2014

We. Are. Home.

    Even as I sit here in my own living room in my favorite chair those words sound surreal.

    It's funny how your priorities come into focus in a crisis. In the past I dreaded international flights with the kids, preparing for every possible scenario and filling my carry-on with a condensed version of Toys R Us. This time, I threw in a few rattles, made sure I had enough diapers and baby food, and hoped for the best.

    What, Virgin Australia? The bulkhead seats with baby bassinets are all taken? I could care less. I would have stood the entire twenty-six hours with Lucy strapped to me if it meant we could go home. Thankfully, Lucy and I both had a seat, and the kind gentleman next to us didn't mind being frequently kicked by a fidgeting sleeper. He didn't mind Lucy either.

    We finally landed, impatiently zigzagged through the customs line, grabbed our suitcases, and then, it was time. The moment I had dreamed about and played out in my head for the last <u>fifty-three days</u>. I rounded the corner, my heart beating out of my chest, and then—well, why don't you just watch for yourself?

    Okay Reader, obviously the video of the Greatest Reunion Ever that I posted on my blog can't pop-up hologram-style from this book. (You should totally go to the blog and watch it though! littlelucymei. blogspot.com, entry title: "Finally Home.") In the meantime, it would be my pleasure to describe it for you as best I can:

Picture me holding Lucy on my hip with one hand and pushing the world's heaviest luggage cart with the other. We exit customs and among the throng I spot those four beautiful faces I've dreamed about for the last two months. They take off running; I take off running, letting go of the luggage cart with reckless abandon. We all crash together in an explosion of sweet relief. *My entire family is in my arms!* But I must get my hands on them one at a time.

Joshua is first. We hold each other tightly, me laughing and heaving sobs simultaneously. There isn't a trace of ten-year-old macho; he's a little boy who's missed his mama and doesn't care who knows it. I think he's grown a foot!

Then comes Sarah Kate, my six-year-old princess who has begged daily for my return, who, as she puts it, "fell asleep lots of nights with my crying face on," because she ached for Lucy and me so much. It's her turn. I sink to the floor, completely unconcerned about the dozens of arriving passengers trying to get by. I envelop her as she buries her face in my neck. Her braids that her Dad made with now expert hands tickle my nose, and it's the greatest feeling in the world. I can't believe I'm really holding her.

Brian meets me on the floor and we cry together. Our faces say, "We did it." I stand on wobbly legs, grab Andrew, and we squeeze as hard as we can. He could not have possibly been smiling any bigger. My lips sink into those soft cheeks and I am in heaven.

I've been holding Lucy this whole time, but Daddy's moment has arrived. This child has been his for two-and-a-half months, yet he was only able to hold her for ten days in China. She's not a tiny, helpless infant anymore. Though he watched her grow through a computer screen, reality is a different story. She's not the same baby he said good-bye to in Guangzhou.

He grieves that he's missed so much, yet rejoices because she thrives. He gently lifts her from my arms and, thankfully, she doesn't protest, a clear answer to prayer. He gifts her with Daddy kisses, making up for two months of precious lost time. I am no longer a single parent. He is no longer a single parent. The burden we've carried for fifty-three days is lifted. Finally, we are complete.

(February 17, 2014 entry continued)

It was one of the happiest days of my whole entire life! "Hope deferred makes the heart sick: but when the desire comes, it is a tree of life" (Proverbs 13:12). In an instant, my sick heart was mended and filled with so much life I felt I was soaring. All of the sleepless nights, the anxiety, the fear of the unknown, the ache for the ones I love the most—it was gone. All that was left was joy. Pure joy.

These last few months there's been a lot of talk about home. Government agencies argued over the definition of home as they deliberated over whether or not Lucy met the permanent resident requirement for automatic citizenship. The title of this blog, "Bringing Lucy Home," which was chosen on a whim, actually became a two-month-long, seemingly impossible trek. "Home" has been the cry of my heart day and night.

Early in this trial, a friend prayed that "the ache you feel for home would remind you of the real soul ache we always have to be with our Savior in heaven."

I know what it feels like to ache for home. When we moved to Australia three years ago, I longed for the familiarity and presence of family and friends. I'd cry and tell Brian, "I want to go home!" meaning America. Fast-forward three years, and I experienced that same ache, but this time it was for Australia, where my husband and babies were.

Neither America nor Australia is a perfect place. As awesome of a job Brian and the kids did with cleaning the house in preparation for my homecoming, today there are more dirty dishes, unmade beds, and clothes to wash. As beautiful as my kids are, they will still argue and test my patience.

As much as I longed to be here, my friend was right. The utmost purpose of that longing was to remind me that I'm not home yet, and I won't be until I reach Heaven, when Jesus will make all things right again. As I long for Heaven, it should not be a mere longing for an absence of pain and suffering. Jesus must be the object of my longing, not just the perfection He offers in eternity.

Simply longing for what Jesus can give me instead of who He is would be as pointless as longing for the furniture in my house instead of my husband and children who live there.

Is it possible for longing to fade? What if, while I was in Memphis, I started to think, "You know, I actually have it pretty good here. My meals are provided for me, I don't have to pay any bills, and it's much easier caring for one child instead of four. I think I'll just stay." That would have been insanity. But isn't that how we get wooed by the pleasures of this world? Instead of simply enjoying the things God gives us and using them for His glory, pretty soon we start to worship them, and the next thing we know, we've forgotten why we're here. We start to think of ourselves as "permanent residents" instead of travelers passing through.

Even though I lived at my parents' house for two months, I kept my clothes in suitcases. I refused to put them in drawers, because I felt like if I did, it would mean I was settling in and staying a while, and in a sense, giving up hope. Instead, I wanted to live each day like it was THE DAY. I wanted to be ready.

Oh, to long for my ultimate home with Jesus with an intensity that surpasses the longing I had for my husband and children. I pray that I will hold this life loosely, living each day as if it were THE DAY that I will finally be Home with Him, for good.

Lucy slept safe and secure in her bed that night, completely unaware of the enormity of the victory her presence in our house represented. To her, it was another night's sleep, just in a different location. To us, her family, it meant the culmination of years of dreaming, doubting, pursuing, fearing, and overcoming. It was the happy ending to months of tears, battles within and without, confusion, and longing. It was the final sentence in the final chapter of our own Book of Suffering: "Lucy and her whole family were finally together and all was right again."

What is the point of suffering? What is the purpose of pain? I can't give a blanket answer to that question, as doing so would minimize the uniqueness of others' trials. I know that our suffering was nothing compared to what others have walked through; therefore, I know I'm not qualified to speak universally. I can only speak for me.

My season of suffering humbled me. It stripped me of idols whose roots were deep, comforts and securities to which I didn't know I clung so tightly. As He did with Elijah, who stood on the mountain and waited for the Lord's presence to pass by, God did not show up in the ways I expected Him to, or demanded Him to. He was not in the wind of imposed deadlines, or the earthquake of public outrage, or the fire of government influence.

Instead, as I stood exposed before my Savior, my demands unmet, and said, "You are enough," He arrived in a quiet whisper, a balm to my parched soul. Echoing His challenge at the beginning of our adoption journey, He said, "Trust me," and I finally did. In a timing that did not match my own, He carried to completion what He began so many years ago and made us a family for good.

Lucy and I stepped onto Australian soil and we were not the same. She was transformed by proper nutrition and love; I was permanently altered by the gift of pain. I arrived broken yet mended, contrite, thankful, and dependent. Big parts of Self had died so Jesus could more fully live in me, and as excruciating as the dying was, my soul says, "More of that, please."

Obedience sometimes equals pain, but always, eventually, equals joy. Bringing Lucy home was one of those offerings of painful obedience.

What a soul-level joy it became.

Finally—the golden ticket. Certificate of Citizenship = Proof required for the passport. We were going home!

PaPaw saying good-bye to his Lucy indefinitely.

The welcome committee gearing up for the big arrival!

Sweet relief. We did it!

Squeezing our girls for the first time in two months.

Chapter 21

What About You?

When we arrived at the Garden Hotel in China, they gave us a backpack for Lucy with all kinds of goodies in it, including a cute little panda bear wearing traditional Chinese clothing. Sarah Kate fell in love with it and was thrilled when we went down to breakfast the next morning and she saw several of the exact same pandas for sale. "Can I get one? Please?" As if we would say no! She loved on "Pandy," as she calls him, slept with him, and lovingly brought him into her inner circle of favorite stuffed animals.

Each morning when we went down to breakfast, Sarah Kate checked on the status of the number of pandas still available, "waiting to be adopted." "Only one left!" she said one morning, but then was dismayed the next day when there were three sitting where there was just one the morning before.

I wanted to tell her that the Garden Hotel has an endless supply of those pandas, and that there will never be none, because the gift shop will just keep re-supplying them each day. I almost told her, but I realized if I did, I would steal her joy of knowing that each panda was going to a loving home. I'd crush her hope of a day when no panda is left waiting for a family.

During the ten days we were in China, I was humbled to be a part of about twenty adoptive families who received their precious children the same time we received our Lucy. I consider these parents my heroes. They enveloped into their family children with heart defects, missing limbs, albinism, and cleft palates, just to name a few of the children's needs.

Those are twenty orphans who are orphans no more. Twenty children who went home with a mom and a dad who will love them, care for them, fight for them, lay down their lives for them. They would have never had a chance if these families had not come.

A cynic might say, "Well, that's twenty out of hundreds of thousands of orphans around the world. That doesn't even make a dent." Yes, this side of heaven, because of the brokenness of this world, there will always be orphans.

The day we adopted Lucy, there was probably another abandoned baby who took her place in that crib, but does this reality lessen the beauty of the fact that Lucy now has a home? That she has a real name, not one assigned to her based on the name of her orphanage? That she has a future with a family who has fallen deeply, madly in love with her? No way.

As I've said before, our journey began when I spent a month in China as a college student and fell in love with the people, and then continued as I worked at a crisis pregnancy center and saw the heartbreaking beauty of adoption from the perspective of the birth mother. God continued to weave our story as He kept adoption before us in different ways and wouldn't let it go, even though we already had three children and had moved across the world from family and friends. He opened the door and said, "Trust Me," even though we were looking at a financial cost we could not imagine affording.

We were fearful of the unknowns, fearful of "messing up our family," fearful of taking on a special needs child when we had three perfectly healthy children—because that's what we all pray for, right? Yet God has shown me that my view of what our lives and our family should be about is so shortsighted. As I've loved on my sweet Lucy who came to us far from healthy at a feeble thirteen pounds, I've been reminded that this story is about something so much bigger—a beautiful picture of God's redemptive story made up of broken pieces, not perfection.

I have been so unbelievably amazed and humbled by the number of people who read my blog and journeyed with us to bring Lucy home. I can never thank you enough for your love and support that brought us through some very hard days.

I cannot end our story without asking, what about you? I can't help but think and pray that maybe, just maybe, the emotion of Lucy's story will not be short-lived, and, instead, some of you may hear God's call to make a journey of your own, a journey of pain and hardship at times, but one of such joy and redemption that you are left undone.

So, where will your story begin? Maybe one day you'll stare in awe at your own adopted child and remember that your journey began when you read a random girl's book about a tiny beauty named Lucy, and God whispered, "There are others."

Yes, there will always be orphans. I weep over this fact. But Lucy is one less, and *she,* my friends, is worth it.

Sources

1. Wikipedia.org/adoption in Australia.
2. www.adoption.state.gov
3. https://www.humanrights.gov.au/sites/default/files/content/
   pdf/social_justice/bringing_them_home_report.pdf.
4. http://www.aph.gov.au/Parliamentary_Business/
   Committees/Senate/Community_Affairs/Completed_
   inquiries/2010-13/commcontribformerforcedadoption/
   report/index
5. http://www.ag.gov.au/FamiliesAndMarriage/
   IntercountryAdoption/Pages/
   Intercountryadoptionpoliciesandkeydocuments.aspx
6. https://movies.yahoo.com/blogs/2013-golden-globes/
   anne-hathaway-describes-filming-dreamed-dream-one-
   les-215521591.html

CPSIA information can be obtained
at www.ICGtesting.com
Printed in the USA
BVHW030250200520
579862BV00003B/340